BROKEN FAMILIES, BROKEN SYSTEMS, BROKEN PROMISES

ROSEMARY BROWN

First published by Ultimate World Publishing 2025
Copyright © 2025 Rosemary Brown

ISBN

Paperback: 978-1-923425-93-4
Ebook: 978-1-923425-94-1

Rosemary Brown has asserted her rights under the Copyright, Designs and Patents Act 1988 to be identified as the author of this work. The information in this book is based on the author's experiences and opinions. The publisher specifically disclaims responsibility for any adverse consequences which may result from use of the information contained herein. Permission to use information has been sought by the author. Any breaches will be rectified in further editions of the book.

All rights reserved. No part of this publication may be reproduced, stored in or introduced into a retrieval system, or transmitted in any form, or by any means (electronic, mechanical, photocopying, recording or otherwise) without the prior written permission of the author. Any person who does any unauthorised act in relation to this publication may be liable to criminal prosecution and civil claims for damages. Enquiries should be made through the publisher.

Cover design: Ultimate World Publishing
Layout and typesetting: Ultimate World Publishing
Editor: Rebecca Low

Ultimate World Publishing
Diamond Creek,
Victoria Australia 3089
www.writeabook.com.au

ACKNOWLEDGEMENTS

I want to acknowledge one very special family—they know who they are. Without their trust and belief in me, this book and **The Inner Compass Code**™ wouldn't have been possible. Thank you from the bottom of my heart.

...Rosemary...

CULTURAL TERMS AND INDIGENOUS WISDOM

This work draws inspiration from diverse cultural traditions—both ancient and contemporary. In particular, terms such as *"men's business", "women's business", "The Dreaming", songlines, dadirri,* and *ngangkari* are respectfully acknowledged as sacred concepts originating from Aboriginal and Torres Strait Islander peoples.

These terms are not explained in depth within this text, as they belong to specific communities, are guided by cultural protocols, and are often part of oral knowledge systems passed through generations. Their inclusion is intended to honour, not interpret or define, these wisdom traditions.

Likewise, references to frameworks such as *Te Whare Tapa Whā* (Māori), *The Sacred Circle* (Native American), and other Indigenous models of wellbeing are included with deep respect for their cultural origins. This book does not claim authority over these frameworks but seeks to recognise their relevance in shaping more holistic, connected understandings of healing.

Where possible, references have been provided to guide readers toward culturally appropriate sources and authors.

TESTIMONIALS

The chaos and stress of addiction were tearing me apart. Alone and afraid, I felt like there was no way out. The constant fear that lived inside me robbed me of any joy and kept me trapped in a relentless cycle of guilt, shame, and despair. I was just as addicted to 'saving' my son from addiction as he was to drugs. Trying to navigate broken systems that too quickly cast our children aside—and overlooking the pain of those who love them—only pushed me closer to breaking point. And then I found Rosemary. Through the simple yet powerful teachings of the Inner Compass, I've learned to step out of the chaos, find my centre, and grow beyond addiction—into a life filled with clarity, peace, and purpose. - MK

When I read a pre-release copy of this book – it was my story on the pages. I thought I was the only one. Eight years of struggles with the system, trying to get help and support, for me and my son. My son had significant mental health issues, he was self-medicating with drugs, and the psychosis was terrifying, but the system never helped, it was like it was easier not to. I met Rosemary by chance, as I was desperately searching for support and answers, it was breaking me. Rosemary and her way of working has empowered me to move forward, my relationship with my son is better and we are all calmer. I feel empowered to now support my son through his struggles, I would hate to think where we would have ended up if we didn't find Rosemary and her traditional ways of **The Inner Compass Code**™. – FP

I had tried everything, you name it - personal development, mental health work, therapy, all kinds of different angles, quantum morphogenetic physics, frequency therapy, even a shaman! I was at the point thinking nothing could help me – and then Rosemary crossed my path. Her ability & her system is hands down the best & most impactful I have ever experienced. Everyone needs to know about this. - PD

DEDICATION

To all those who have willingly shared the raw, unvarnished truth of their journey.

To the families, brave souls, weary hearts, and determined spirits who entrusted me to stand beside them, to serve and support when the path felt too heavy to walk alone.

This book and **The Inner Compass Code**™ are dedicated to you.

It's your story—your struggles, triumphs, fierce love, and unbreakable hope—that lives within these pages.

Your courage to let me walk alongside you has shaped every word, insight, and compass point within this work. Without you, none of this could exist.

May these pages honour your journey. May they carry forward the wisdom you've gifted me. And may *The Inner Compass Code*™ continue to light the way, not just for you, but for all those still searching for their way home.

With deepest respect,
Rosemary

CONTENTS

Acknowledgements   iii
Cultural Terms and Indigenous Wisdom   v
Testimonials   vii
Dedication   ix
Prologue   1
Introduction   3

PART ONE: It All Started with Me   5
Chapter One: A Stolen Voice   7
Chapter Two: Acknowledging My Core Self   13
Chapter Three: Slipping Into Alcohol   23
Chapter Four: Only Knowing What I Knew   35
Chapter Five: The Battlefield of Sanity   45

PART TWO: What Doesn't Work And Why   51
Chapter One: The System   55
Chapter Two: Ivory Towers and Pedestals   67
Chapter Three: The Destruction of Culture   85
Chapter Four: Role Modelling and Influencers   101
Chapter Five: The Erosion of Empowerment   113

PART THREE: The Urgency of Change   127
Chapter One: Ancient Foundation, Modern Compass   131
Chapter Two: From Disempowerment to Empowerment   143

Chapter Three: A New Way of Working	151
Chapter Four: Words Shape Worlds – Labels Shape Lives	159
Chapter Five: The Fire Within	167
Conclusion	175
The Compass Is Yours Now	175
About The Author	179
Disclaimer	185
References	187

PROLOGUE

This was the straw that broke the camel's back. The final nail in the coffin, and there was death in mind. Words were ringing in my ears; words that meant there was no point to life anymore.

Through the turmoil and chaos of pain and heartbreak, it only took a split second to make the decision. It's time, I'm ready. I no longer needed to battle to stay alive; the thoughts that were ever present in my life had finally been given the permission to act.

The sense of relief I felt was calming; it stilled my mind. I had an action plan, and now I just needed the strength to carry out my own suicide.

All I needed was a very large bottle of bourbon to take away any fear of the physical pain I might feel that would stop me from following through. I had a plan, and it was time I acted on it.

Standing on the front deck of my home, looking across at the little retail centre that would assist me in this act, I felt relieved that I didn't have to drive anywhere and delay my actions. There was a bottle shop within less than a minute's walk, and I had my shoes on, wallet in hand.

Head hung low, I opened the gate onto the footpath and took another step into my plan, a plan that would free me from the hurt, pain, and horrendous thoughts I often had.

My desire to kill myself was finally going to be met; it seemed like a dream come true.

I stumbled to cross the road; I didn't want anyone to see my tears. I felt a resolve; I was willing myself to hurry, so I could get this over and done with.

I had only taken three steps when I heard a voice asking, "Rosemary, are you alright?"

Startled, I looked up. Whose voice was this asking this foreign question?

Through my tears, I recognised the blurred face of my doctor standing outside the doctor's surgery. Bewildered, my thoughts raced. What was she doing here? She never stands out in front of the surgery. Something wasn't right; she didn't fit here.

I was confused as I looked back at her, knowing I wasn't alright, knowing I didn't care if I lived or died. I stood frozen in stunned silence, unsure of what the next words would be for me.

INTRODUCTION

Some stories begin with hope. Mine began with collapse—the kind that hollows you out and leaves only silence in its wake.

If you've just read the prologue, you'll know the truth of where this journey started: not with a fresh start, but with a soul implosion. A moment so final, even the wind seemed to hold its breath. And yet, through the fog of tears and the crushing weight of despair, something shifted. Not in a blaze of glory. Not in a neatly scripted plot twist. But in a single, soul-stilling moment where a voice—unexpected and uninvited—asked if I was alright.

This book was born from that question.

It's not a book about labels or diagnoses. It's not bound to one story, one struggle, or one kind of pain. It's, at its heart, a book about **awakening**—about reclaiming a voice long silenced, a spirit long shackled, and a purpose buried beneath other people's expectations.

For decades, I walked beside those caught in chaos—mothers, sons, professionals, lovers—each one facing storms the world couldn't always see. I offered them lifelines while quietly unravelling myself. My strength was mistaken for certainty, my knowledge for power. Yet inside, I often stood on unstable ground, questioning my place, my worth, and the path I was forging.

This book is my truth. Not the polished kind. The kind that bleeds, scars, and heals again. It's stitched with stories from the frontlines, of pain, yes, but also of breathtaking transformation, deep human resilience, and the courage it takes to stop performing and start becoming.

It's also a mirror.

You may find your own shadows reflected here—your doubts, regrets, and untold aches. But you'll also find hope. A thread, however fine, that leads toward something steadier, clearer, and more rooted. This isn't a manual. It's a **compass**—one that doesn't promise perfection, but direction.

I don't write as someone who has figured it all out. I write as someone who finally stopped trying to fit a life shaped by others' definitions of success, healing, or worth. And in doing so, I found my voice—not just for me, but for others ready to rise, reclaim, and remember who they are beneath the chaos.

So, if you've ever felt invisible in the very place you were meant to be seen.

If you've been told you're too much, too intense, too soft, too wild, too anything.

If you've held the pieces together for everyone else while secretly falling apart yourself.

This book is for you.
Welcome aboard.
The storm may rage, but there's a lighthouse on the horizon.

Let's begin...

PART ONE

IT ALL STARTED WITH ME

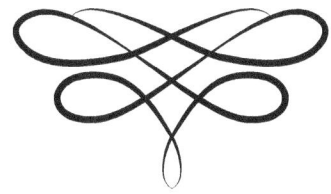

Before the systems.

Before the theories, frameworks, and names I would one day carry, there was just me.

A woman. A daughter. A partner. A mother. Trying to keep the pieces together. Trying not to fall apart.

This part of the book doesn't begin with credentials. It begins with a confession: I didn't set out to be a changemaker. I set out to survive.

What follows isn't the story of someone who had it all figured out and then fell from grace. It's the story of someone who was never quite sure who she was *allowed* to be in the first place. A woman shaped by generations of silence, loyalty, and self-sacrifice. A woman who lived in service of everyone else's needs until the weight of it became unbearable.

These early chapters trace the terrain of my inner world—the quiet hurts I carried, the roles I performed, and the moments I lost myself trying to be everything to everyone. You'll see the slow unravel. The ache beneath the mask. The storms I tried to outpace, outrun, out-drink.

But you'll also see something else. The flickers. The questions. The stubborn spark that refused to go out. The moment I realised that if I wanted anything to truly change, I had to begin with me.

This isn't the beginning of the *end* of the story. This is the beginning of a reckoning. The first true step on a path that was never paved, but carved by courage, collapse, and ultimately, a calling I could no longer ignore.

It all started with me. And perhaps, that's where it must start for you, too.

Chapter One

A STOLEN VOICE

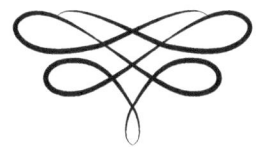

"When the world goes silent, your soul learns to scream."

I came into this world lost and alone. My cries seemed to vanish into thin air—unheard, unnoticed. My early memories are like elusive ghosts, much like most of my childhood recollections. No matter how tightly I close my eyes, something unseen blocks my path back in time. All I know is that, from the very beginning, I've struggled.

As the lonely third child in my family, born four years after my brother and eight years after my eldest sister, I often wonder if I was planned or if I simply arrived, quietly developing after a fleeting moment between my parents. I felt adrift, alone on a journey no one else seemed to understand.

Unhappiness was my constant companion, a dark veil wrapped around my heart, one I couldn't seem to lift. They saw it. They sensed it. But they never truly heard the cries of my soul. Everyone just accepted it: *"That's just how she is."*

I'm the little girl inside the grown-up Rosemary, telling this story through the eyes of a child. As a young girl, I couldn't grasp the chaos and turmoil around me. With my child's mind, in my child's body, none of it made sense, so it settled deep inside me as confused, wordless baggage. Bewildered and unable to find the language for what I felt, I stayed silent.

From such a young age, I grappled with heavy questions, searching for words to express my struggles, longing and quietly aching to belong. Could others not see this? Or did they only see a sad, angry, frustrated child? My memories of growing up are few, yet deep down, I'm still that little girl.

One memory often returns to me. I was preschool age, sitting lost and alone on a trailer in the neighbour's paddock. The heartbreak I felt gripped every part of my being. With tear-filled eyes, I hugged my knees to my chest and gazed at the farmer, who continued his tractor work, oblivious to my distress, my broken heart.

That little girl had been so excited earlier, eagerly awaiting the moment I could hop in the car with Dad and head to a very special place. It was calf-club day at the local primary school, a day everyone looked forward to—especially me. I kept my excitement hidden, afraid that if they knew how much I cared, they might not let me go, or something might happen to spoil it.

In my mind, I pictured the sprawl of creative gems the kids would bring: lambs, calves, and exquisite works of art like sand saucers, posies, floating bowls, miniature gardens, and best of all, animals made from vegetables. I couldn't wait to see these wonders.

In my dreams, I saw children clapping with joy, beaming as they pulled their parents to admire their masterpieces, a proud little card saying *"First Prize"* adding to their glow. I imagined myself arriving one day with my beautifully prepared calf and my amazing creations, ribbons placed around my calf's neck by the judges, and a gleam of pride lighting up my face.

But that day, my excitement and dreams were shattered. No one noticed my distress. No one tried to make it better. Unaware of the dark place my emotions had slipped into, I took another step into unhappiness and anger—another step away from people, drawing even closer to animals.

From the beginning, animals were my soulmates. They looked into my eyes, and I into theirs, and I found acceptance in their soft, kind gazes. The comfort and solace I longed for from humans were freely given to me by animals. Words weren't needed. They knew. They felt it. They gave without expectation, judgment, or criticism.

Animals listened. They snuggled close when I cried. The farm dog would do its best to wipe away my tears with a lick, serving as a makeshift flannel. My inner child remembers the comfort of sitting in the paddock with my horse, sharing all my woes, while the dogs rested their heads on my knees, looking up with love in their beautiful, soft brown eyes.

Back on the trailer, I later learnt that my parents had rushed my younger sister to the hospital after she swallowed a threepence—a tiny silver coin—that had lodged in her windpipe. As a toddler, all I could see was my little sister ruining my life again. I felt so alone. No one noticed me. They just went on with their day. Beyond my initial distress, I have no memory of how I got off that trailer or returned to my usual life. Inside, I played the role I was learning, finding comfort in the company of animals rather than people.

I had believed in fairytales, in the perfect princess dreams spun from stories of how wonderful life could be. But reality shattered those dreams into painful, hurtful pieces—each shard building the tower of anger and sadness I began to inhabit. A pyramid of injustice, growing with each disappointment.

Reflecting as an adult, I realise my childhood had its moments of greatness, but it was also a confusing maze. After that calf-club day, I was already making rules for myself: *no one cares*, *no one notices*. A core belief took root:

If you're not feeling okay,
you have to figure it out on your own.

As a child, I searched everywhere for that magical someone—someone who understood, who could help me out of the deep, dark place I often found myself in when my dreams were crushed. Other moments in my childhood only reinforced these rules: *You're on your own*.

I remember pedalling my bicycle up a steep hill on the way to school when a flash of reality hit me like a wave, filling me with dread. I was desperate to get through the day without anyone noticing me. I thought invisibility would keep me safe. But deep inside, there was an ache—a hope that someone would see me for who I truly was beneath the hardening shell.

Suddenly, a picture returned—me, lying on cold, hard concrete, surrounded by children cheering or shouting. My throat was tight. A weight pressed against my chest, and I struggled to draw breath. I was five years old, trying to scream, but no sound came out.

The weight on my chest belonged to an older girl. Her hands were around my throat, squeezing tight, cutting off my air. Her face loomed above me, cold and unrelenting, her eyes dark with intent. She was close to finishing what she had started.

The feelings etched into my heart that day—pain, helplessness, confusion, and the unbearable silence as no one helped—added fuel to my fire of anger and injustice. At five years old, I knew I had to toughen up. I began building a shield of steel around myself.

A teacher, hearing the commotion, pulled the girl off me. But once again, I have no memory of what happened next. I'm sure someone must have cared enough to check if I was okay…but the rules I created to survive still echo through my life. They were forged early, and fiercely: *You're alone. Be strong. Trust no one to rescue you.*

My mind blocked out the good things. Those feelings were fleeting, too fragile to hold. One clear memory shines through—sitting in class when man landed on the moon in 1969. *Apollo 11. Neil Armstrong.* "One small step for man, one giant leap for mankind." I felt the miracle of it. It felt like anything was possible—for others.

But soon, I was pulled back into my dark hole—a place no one ever explored with me. Lost and alone. Not truly belonging. Never being heard.

Later childhood events only deepened these feelings. I often recall my mother's frustration with me, fuelled by what I now understand to be her illness—and my own frustration, fuelled by a desperate need to be noticed and understood.

Chapter Two

ACKNOWLEDGING MY CORE SELF

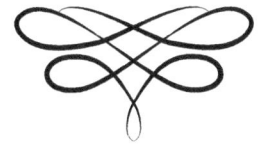

"The journey home begins with a whisper from within."

I wasn't born with a book on how to handle life on life's terms. I came into this world clueless about so many things. Looking back now, I see that I inherited many values, beliefs, and ways of acting from my parents and those close to me as I grew up.

My dad was the most amazing man in my life. He was kind, and I was his favourite—or at least it felt that way. He treated me like he understood me. Or maybe that was just a child's fantasy, a dream I clung to. Maybe he did understand. Or maybe he didn't.

As a teenager, I began to understand more about my father's trauma as a World War II veteran and the tragedies he endured. No man should have to face the losses my father faced. I'm sure that, as a child feeling so close to him, I absorbed his silence and some of his pain.

No one ever really knew what went on inside this incredible man. He must have been overwhelmed with shock and grief at his wife's passing. Or maybe his stoic exterior didn't allow those emotions in, holding them at bay with an invisible shield. Either way, I absorbed that silence. It became part of me, too.

Now, as an adult reflecting on my own beliefs and where they come from, I see this story about my parents as a kind of internal flashcard. It appears every time I find myself thinking, *you need to toughen up.*

Dad was married when he went off to war. He had a wife and two children, and his wife was expecting their third child when he said goodbye. I can't imagine what he must have felt as he boarded that boat, headed to his posting as a soldier.

Soon after he left, his wife died from an infection after giving birth. It wasn't the birth that killed her but the infection, and there was no penicillin to fight the bacteria. It was wartime, and those life-saving drugs were reserved for the war effort.

He had just four days to come home, bury his wife, and make arrangements for his three children, one just a newborn. His mother and sister stepped in as a temporary solution, and on the fourth day, he was back to war, dealing with his loss in a battle-torn landscape.

I can only imagine the heartbreak, desperation, and anguish that must have been sheer hell for my father—a hell he kept hidden from prying eyes all his life.

Broken Families, Broken Systems, Broken Promises
Acknowledging My Core Self

My mum was a tall, striking woman with dark hair. The story goes that she was full of fun, excitement, and joy. But that was all ripped away in a split second when she read a little sheet of paper. It came in a plain brown envelope on green paper with grey, wonky letters spelling out the wartime message.

Her first real love, her fiancé, was an American soldier who matched her in stature and strength and shared her excitement, hopes, and dreams for their future together. But war ensured that those dreams would never become a reality. Like a grenade exploding in her heart, my mum's life changed forever with a telegram that delivered the cold, hard news that he had died in the heat of battle.

I can only imagine the overwhelming shock, the crushing feeling of loss and loneliness that would have come over her. I never heard my mum or dad speak of these events, or of the two people they lost during the war, leaving them both alone.

Both my parents were raised during the Great Depression, when things were scarce and money was hard to come by. World War II changed all that, creating a vibrant economy across the globe, with so many jobs and so few workers to produce the things necessary for war. The war changed the world in so many ways, tearing apart lives and creating unknown paths forward.

Even though the horrors of war were never talked about, I feel like the impact of that war has been passed down in my genes. I have an intimate connection to the suffering war brought to the generations before me, or maybe I was there in another space and time. The silence spun itself around me like thread—light at first, then binding.

So many people went through those war years with their lives torn apart, receiving devastating news in a little brown envelope with a window on the front. Inside, a brief, factual telegram: *"It is with regret we inform you of the death of..."* often read alone. Many carried the internal scars from war, but very few spoke of its horrors. Some turned to alcohol to cope, while others struggled on for years, until death finally released them from the clutches of trauma and grief. These things were ingrained in their spirits and genes—the historical trauma passed down to the next generation.

My dad never spoke of the war or the nightmare of his losses, nor did my mum. The only story I remember is of my mum being rescued by the Salvation Army on a train station platform. She was lost and alone, having what others called a "nervous breakdown." After that, my parents always donated to the Salvation Army.

This story is important for me to tell because it sets the scene for who I am today. You might also recognise the lingering nature of PTSD. These wartime heroes who survived had to learn to cope with their demons on their own. Back then, you had no choice but to get on with life. Some did that in healthy ways, others not so much.

The resilience my father showed became a foundation for me as a little girl. Without even knowing it, I started to build my own resilience to the unfairness of life.

We never needed many words. Sometimes just sitting beside him while he tinkered with something—his quiet presence wrapped around me like a blanket—was all the comfort I needed. The silence of my father's pain was as loud as a sonic boom, but I respected that silence. It was comforting to me, too.

Somehow, Mum and Dad came together and married. I dream they both shared a vision for their future together—a positive future free from the noise of war, full of hard work, joy, hopes, and dreams.

But I've learned that reality is often the opposite of what I used to dream. Reality is cold, hard, and it hurts. Demons creep into reality, feeding on happiness until it's all gone. They seem bent on destroying dreamers and their hearts and souls.

It certainly seemed that way for my mum and dad. They started their life together, probably dreaming of a honeymoon and joy. They had a small, remote farm in a place called Utiku in New Zealand. The land was rough and hard; it needed a lot of work to become productive. There was no machinery—just bare hands and hard work. One thing I inherited from my dad was a strong work ethic. His voice still rings in my head today: *"If a job's worth doing, it's worth doing well,"* and *"Do it once, do it right!"*

Nothing was spoken; there might have just been an assumption that everything would work out. Married, and hey presto, three ready-made children. All strangers in a strange place, a strange home, and a strange land, with no familiar family.

These children were lost and alone, too, having struggled through the war years with no guiding hand from their father or mother. Their struggles went unheard, and in their tiny minds, their father was away at war and could die, too.

Coming together as strangers, all carrying their own wartime trauma, must have felt like sitting on a cliff during a massive earthquake—the ground shaking, thoughts racing, the fear of not knowing what would come next. Everyone trying to keep their absolute terror at bay.

The shock must have been enormous. I guess being reunited with their dad, knowing their mother was dead, and seeing a new woman in a rough-built home didn't go down too well with the kids. They were trying to cope and make sense of their lives.

Mum struggled too—her trauma and nervous breakdowns robbing her of emotional stability. I can imagine that feeling—wanting to be strong but incapable of keeping it together.

The once-bright picture of hope soon lost its colour and excitement. A sense of doom crept in. Something needed to be done. Dad made what I can only call a decision made in desperation. He arranged for the two eldest children to be adopted by another family and the youngest to be adopted by his sister and her husband.

Another grenade exploded in everyone's lives, and no one could escape the damage or the impact of this blast. The story is that Dad didn't tell his children—he just drove the two eldest to the west coast and left them to figure it out with these people they didn't know.

I've reflected on these things with my oldest half-brother before he died. He and I connected well; he understood and had empathy. I don't think the other two were ever able to put their life experiences in context, either at a head level or an internal level.

Silence has been golden over the years in our family. I never knew I had two half-brothers and a half-sister until I was 16 years old.

My younger sister asked who the man who used to visit every now and then was, and it turned out he was our youngest half-brother.

So many people endured such things during and after the war. My connection isn't sympathy but empathy—trying to understand the reality and struggles those people faced amid tragedy. Others without such empathy sought to criticise and judge.

I was watching a documentary the other week. It told the story of a woman who was adopted at a very young age. She was seeking to know her biological father and find out if he was a "good man." In her journey, she heard many amazing stories about her father and was able to put him on a pedestal—what a great and amazing dad she had missed out on knowing.

Wow. She even met a half-sister she didn't know existed—one who grew up with her father and who recounted a story similar to my father's. He, too, had faced what I believe must have been a gut-wrenching decision to give up his children from an earlier relationship to be adopted by another family.

But then, something changed. The tone shifted. And I watched how quickly the pedestal was ripped out from under her father's frame. How quickly he dropped to the floor—and went further down—as she began judging him as "a bad dad." No acceptance of the reality of the time. No questions about the circumstances. Just the judgment that he was "bad" because he had given her up for adoption.

She judged her father harshly because he made what he believed was the right decision for his children at the time. Watching life go by through my eyes, I recognise how easily others judge or criticise when compassion would be much more appropriate.

This sickened me. It's a familiar feeling I carry with me today. How dare people judge others by their standards, with no connection to reality, no empathy, no thoughts for those who care about them and the struggles that led to a massive decision that impacted the lives of others.

I know that sometimes doing the "right" thing isn't always going to be regarded by others as okay. I have grown to accept:

"No one ever does less than their best, given the reality at the time, given the skills they have, and the emotional impact on their lives."

That applies even to the person who just stabbed their neighbour. At that time, that was the best they could do. That's not to say it was okay—it's not okay to stab someone. It's saying that's the best that person could do at the time, and if they don't like the impact of that on their life, they need to seek help to change.

Growing up, I recognised the righteousness of others, believing that they're holier than thou and have the right to demean and criticise others.

Dad's coping mechanism was to not talk about the past. His father had been an alcoholic, and Dad rarely drank, as I think he feared becoming someone he didn't want to be if he had too many. The war and the impact of his losses had stolen his voice. I think that's where Dad and I connected—in the silence of our reality.

Mum never really connected with me. In my memory, my mum was always unwell, and I was always angry. My anger over the years overtook my sadness. I've since discovered these feelings go back lifetimes for me, as do my sense of unfairness and injustice.

As I reflect, I recognise that my "little girl" self—over my childhood and the difficult times I faced—became trapped by demon soul-eating spiders, leaving my angels of grace and gratitude far from my reach.

This web soon became the foundation of my existence.

Chapter Three

SLIPPING INTO ALCOHOL

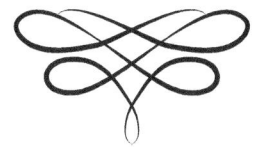

"What numbs the pain, also deepens the wound."

At 14, I was a bit of a rebel—angry, hurt, and misunderstood. They call it bullying today, but back then, I was abused. Because of that, my mum struggled with my desperate, adapted behaviours. She saw me as a *problem,* while my dad was my best friend. Alongside him, my horses and dog were my closest companions.

Loss seemed to be the theme as I entered my teenage years. One day, I was biking home from school when my darling Melissa—my little wire-haired fox terrier—came running out to greet me. She was so happy. Just as she reached me, our neighbour rounded the corner in their car. The brakes screeched, and I jumped off my bike, but it was over in an instant. Melissa was hit and died right before my eyes. I must have been only 10, maybe 11.

Then there was Flicker, my first pony. She broke her sesamoid bone, and I came home to find the huntsman's truck in the driveway, ready to take my cherished Flicker away for slaughter—meat for the hounds. I could only imagine her, strung from a sturdy tree, her body carved out for ravenous dogs. I was devastated. And furious.

Over a cup of tea, the huntsman said he'd keep her and breed from her. Dad decided that if the huntsman could do that, then so could we. Flicker ended up in foal to the teaser stallion at Santa Rosa Stud, and little Gem was born—a happy time for everyone in the family.

Looking back, I can see how much I struggled to be accepted by others. I never felt like I truly belonged. I was always hopeful—always wanting to be liked—but I ended up an easy target for teasing and bullying. And let me tell you, when you're swimming in a pool of anger, every new wound just keeps that pool filled to overflowing.

It's funny how patterns repeat themselves over the years. Even now, I struggle with being accepted. Or maybe it's just that I'm different. I've come to recognise just how different I am from everyone else.

I remember one evening, in an online group I run, we were discussing the topic of the "homeless addict." One of the greatest fears for those who love someone with addiction is the worry that, if they end up homeless, they won't survive. I asked the group to reflect on how well they could look after themselves at 14.

Most of the group—mainly mothers and grandparents with children in addiction—shared stories of being "good," of doing as they were told, of not questioning their parents. One mum had to grow up quickly, raising her siblings without adult support.

When it was my turn, I shared a different story—one filled with anger, chaos, and drama. I was drinking, being promiscuous, and never fitting in. But despite all that, I was always a high achiever. I worked hard and excelled at school, even more than my siblings.

I topped school certificate in biology and came second in maths. Who would've thought? I didn't study much because I knew that if I listened in class—when I wasn't skipping—I could retain the information. I had a knack for just *knowing* the answers.

I never stressed about exams. I never thought I'd fail—and to this day, the only exam I've ever failed was a law paper I took at tech school. That's why I'm not a lawyer! Everything I did—whether studying or writing essays—was already mapped out in my head, sometimes for weeks or even months. Even when I wrote my first book, it was all there inside me; I just had to put it on paper.

I had so much time to think in my teenage years. I'd often ride my horse down to the river, just the two of us, solving all of life's problems. My dog, too, was there for many of the courtroom hearings I imagined in my head, where I felt judged and misunderstood. My dog's answer was always the same: be silent, snuggle in close, and make it all feel right.

But everything wasn't right inside, and I think Dad knew that. As a young teen, I was lucky to have him. He let me go off on my own—rabbit shooting, working the land, doing the farm stuff I loved. I remember the .22 rifle at the end of my bed, ready to shoot the early morning bunnies from my bedroom window. I wasn't a bad shot from the kitchen window either.

I had a great life growing up on the farm. I had freedom. I didn't have to stay inside with Mum or my sister. I knew how to look after myself, and in those days, not much "bad stuff" happened to kids—or at least, no one talked about it if it did.

But my teenage years brought more pain, trauma, and injustice. I worked hard, and soon I learned to play hard. I was 14 when I started drinking—working in a man's world and learning to drink like one.

Shearing was a tough job; there was none of the safety gear you see today. As a roustabout, it was hard, physical work. But I was reliable, I worked hard, and I pushed myself—dragging sheep out for the shearers, learning how to shear, and setting up my future in an environment where, at last, I felt I belonged.

I carried my reputation well. By 16, I could drink most men under the table. I shudder to think of the amount of alcohol I consumed. Still, no one noticed—and if they did, they never said anything. It suited me fine back then, but looking back now, all the signs of a child on a high-risk path were there. I threw myself further into an unhealthy lifestyle.

I remember being 14 or 15, meeting my first boyfriend at the local rodeo. We sat on top of the cattle truck crates, drinking who knows how many bottles of beer. Back then, we didn't count bottles—we counted crates.

Mum and Dad were meant to pick me up, and my first beau walked me to the car. I can still picture it now: Dad in the driver's seat of our white Holden Kingswood, listening to Mr Handsome leaning on his knees, swaying in the breeze, asking if he could take me out again.

I sat in the back seat, window down, trying not to breathe on anyone—I was drunker than ever. I'm not sure what Dad said, but I know my boyfriend would later drive up to where I lived and sit in his car down the road, too nervous to come in. I wouldn't go out to see him; I'd just sit at my bedroom window, smoking a cigarette, wishing he would. I think Dad eventually told him that if he wanted to see me, he needed to come in, not just sit out on the road.

At school, I was there to achieve. I often left early, saying I needed to catch the bus home—we lived 20 kilometres away. No one questioned it. I would go to my younger sister's class and pick her up most days for an early escape.

I had a great friend at school whose dad was a vet. They were really into horses, and whenever I could, I'd go to her place. I was never a brilliant rider, but I gave it my all. Throughout my teenage years, I pushed every boundary and got away with most of it. All I wanted was to fit in, to be admired, to have people call me their friend.

My teachers didn't see it either. To them, I was a challenge. I was defiant. My grades were high, but my behaviour clearly showed I was a troubled teen in pain.

Looking back, I realise no one truly saw my potential. I never saw any limitations for myself, no matter how I was feeling or what emotional storm I was caught in. I just became more determined to succeed.

Give me a job, and I'd do it. I was often relied upon to lead, to take on adult responsibilities. I became a pony club instructor at 15—not because I was asked, but because no one else would. Stepping up became second nature, especially when it came to work while I was still at school.

I recognised empathy in others who struggled, because I understood what it felt like to struggle. I'd be there—not to fix them, just to listen, so they knew someone cared.

When you know what a broken heart feels like, when you understand trauma and sadness, when you've had to "be tough," you become something rare. You understand the reality of life. I always knew I was different. I always felt like I didn't quite fit. And I was drawn to others who didn't fit, either.

It's heartbreaking to realise that today, so many young people are in the same boat—full of talent, but hurting, angry, and drowning in pain. No one sees them. The signs are all there, but people just label them as "bad." I understand their behaviours may be destructive, but I also recognise the absence of elders, guidance, and the harsh judgment placed on them by the community.

My nana was amazing. She would drive the 20 kilometres to the farm every Sunday for a traditional roast lunch. I admired my nana. Her green Vauxhall Velox was a massive car for such a little old lady, with a long bench seat and column shift gear. I'm still in awe of her resilience and determination. She always achieved whatever she set out to do.

However, Nana had her moments of struggle, too. I remember once finding her sitting in front of the kitchen fire, tears rolling down her cheeks. Mum—her daughter—had said or done something to make her feel unwelcome. I sat beside her, held her hand, and simply let her be sad. I knew what it felt like to be unwanted. My heart went out to her.

The thing is—I *knew* I had a caring heart. Nana saw it. Dad saw it too. But to everyone else, I was just an angry teenager who didn't fit their mould of what a good daughter, sister, or friend should be.

And speaking of fitting in, my first boyfriend wasn't genuine. He had another girlfriend while he was seeing me. That pattern has repeated throughout my life. I seemed to attract men who wanted to play with me and every other girl who crossed their path.

Loving animals was my salvation. I connected with those who struggled, and those two things—animals and empathy—shaped my passion for the future. I also loved trucks. When I thought about life after school, I wanted to be a truck driver, a vet, or—believe it or not—a policewoman.

Back then, truck driving wasn't seen as a job for women. Every company I approached turned me down. I had my HT licence. I wasn't meek or mild—in fact, I was strong and capable—yet no one wanted to give me a chance.

Becoming a vet was another dream. But vet school was hard to get into—just as it is today—and my parents didn't support me pursuing it. So that dream ended before it began.

I even wanted to take over the family farm. But again, my parents didn't support me. I was crushed when my older sister and her husband—a draftsman in forestry, not even a farmer—came to take over. He knew nothing about farming or animal care, yet Dad took the time to train him.

Why did no one ever believe in me? After everything I'd done to help Dad on the farm, it felt like the ultimate betrayal. But one thing I've never lost is my belief in *myself*. I knew I'd find a way. I dug deep and kept going.

Instead, I pursued my goal of becoming a policewoman. I was 18, and back then, there were only four spots for women in each intake, and the selection process was tough. Interviews, written tests, character checks, fitness assessments—determination was everything.

I made it to the final six women and was told to come back the following year, as I was one of the youngest to get that far. One thing that stuck with me was what the recruitment officer told me. When they interviewed my mum, she told them I hung out with the "wrong" crowd. He asked me why, and I told him something I still believe to this day:

> **"I trust these people. The so-called 'right' people will let you down or stab you in the back without a second thought. The people I hang with have my back. They'll catch me if I fall."**

My teenage years taught me so much about injustice—that what you see isn't always what you get. Many judged me without knowing me, and they didn't care if they were wrong. This pattern has continued through my life. I guess there's something about me that challenges others. I stand up for what *I* believe is right, not what the world tells me is right.

It's hard to find your way in a world full of ambiguous signs—stumbling from one life event to the next. Alcohol dulled the ache inside me. It gave me a short break from the thoughts that haunted me. Deep down, there was a hollow space within me that cried out to be seen, valued, and loved.

Confusion reigned. Those nagging thoughts that whispered, *There's something wrong with you.* Yet even when those thoughts grew louder—*Life's too hard. It's not worth living* I didn't believe them. I wanted to speak, to tell someone, but the words froze in my throat. My brain whispered, *What's the point? They won't get it.*

Loneliness was my constant companion because how *can* you fit in when you're "different"—when others don't see you, don't recognise your value, or understand your struggles?

As it turned out, most of my friends were older than I. My craving for affection sent me down a dark path, seeking connection in all the wrong places. My only link with boys or men came from giving them what they wanted, regardless of what *I* wanted.

Tired of needing validation from others, I drifted into a lifestyle of drinking and fleeting relationships. I was a good student academically, but a "bad" student in terms of behaviour. Getting good marks was easy, but emotionally, I received no positive feedback for simply being me.

I spent hours alone—sad and lost—wandering out to be with my horse or my dog, crying silently into their fur. As one of them softly nuzzled me, I felt a depth of genuine caring that I had never experienced from another human being. That kind of quiet, unconditional caring has always been what animals have given me throughout my life.

Smiling and laughing often escaped me. Every time I was teased or ridiculed for my lack of joy, I shrank further into my inner black hole. Anger joined me there—a long-standing companion since childhood—sitting heavily in the pit of my stomach, ready to lash out at anything and everything, just to relieve the pressure.

As I moved into my late teens and early adulthood, my drinking didn't subside. I felt like I *belonged* with other drinkers. I belonged on a bar stool or sitting on a beer crate at the local pub. Life was on autopilot. I wasn't able to fulfil any of my dreams—I felt pushed into becoming someone others thought I *should* be.

I remember the day my mother announced that I couldn't work in a shearing gang forever. She had arranged an interview for a "proper" job. I got it—and I remember thinking, *Crap, I don't want to spend my days in an office. There's no freedom in that!* But there was an upside: it was my first real job and my first opportunity to leave home and spread my wings. I did well at work, but I hated the hypocrisy I saw every day. My supervisor was a man of strong religious faith, yet he never stopped criticising me and my lifestyle.

He triggered many of the beliefs I'd absorbed from Sunday School and Wednesday night Bible classes. Those nights, filled with stories of what happened to sinners—tales of heaven, hell, and eternal judgment—I hated them. I'd ride my bike home as fast as

I could. When asked why I hadn't been at Bible class, I'd simply say, "I forgot," and escape through the back door into the safety of the farm and the comfort of my animals.

That little girl imagined being hurled into the jaws of hell—consumed by brimstone and fire—a bad, bad human, steeped in sin, destined to die. I smirk a little as I write this now. The devil and hell haven't caught me yet. Over time, I've come to believe that religion is man-made, built on power and control. God isn't bad. God, to me, is love and caring. It's man who distorts that, who craves power and casts judgment, using God's name to justify the very worst of things.

If there *is* a heaven and a hell, then surely, we already live in hell. From what I've seen, this world is full of suffering and evil. And yet, for some, it's also a place of love, beauty, kindness—a heaven on Earth. Maybe it's both, depending on where we are in life.

I've learned that life is, in many ways, what we make of it. But I also know that, at 20 years old, when I finally set off overseas to pursue my dreams of freedom and travel, the inevitable clash between dreams and reality would shatter everything I believed. It smashed my world into a million shards of broken glass.

Months passed, and I was working on a 20,000-acre property in northern New South Wales. It was eye-opening—a world away from the familiar farming life I had known in New Zealand. Sitting astride a strong bay mare, I felt the light tickle of a swarm of flies settling on my cheek. Sweat ran in rivulets down my neck, trickling along my spine—the only moisture in that vast, sunbaked land.

I was at one with my horse. She was full of energy, adrenaline pulsing through her veins, just as it coursed through mine. Everything was coming together. We were separating cows and calves—a thrilling task, with no fences or boundaries to contain our movement. Spurring my horse to cut off a cow that had broken from the herd, I was laser-focused on stopping her from returning to her calf.

I reined my horse in close on the cow's shoulder, trying to turn her back, to force her away. My entire being focused on cutting her off. Horse and cow collided—both at full gallop—and in an instant, everything went black.

When light returned, I saw nurses. White sheets. A hospital bed. Pain. Then darkness again.

This was to be another turning point in my life.
At 20 years old, nothing would ever be the same again.

Chapter Four

ONLY KNOWING WHAT I KNEW

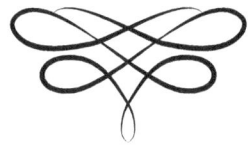

"You can't see the truth until you realise you've been blind."

I'm not sure if we ever really know what we need or how to find it. I was never certain if there was any real purpose or meaning in my life. It seemed like everything I tried to do ended up in a mess. It was as if there was a cliff at every turn, and I just kept stumbling right over it.

After my accident, I had no choice but to return home. I remember it so clearly: me, the horse, the cow, and a couple of calves were all thrown into the air, only to come crashing down to earth in a chaotic heap. Gravity is a cruel force, and when you hit the ground with a thud, surrounded by four bodies and 16 legs flailing around and on top of you, injury is almost a certainty. They say if it hadn't been for one of my bosses getting there in time, I probably wouldn't have survived.

When I finally came to, I was in a hospital bed, my dreams of travelling the world and experiencing life put on hold once again. But somehow, my determination to survive got me from that hospital bed back to the farm, and then onto a plane back to New Zealand. My instincts to survive were strong, giving me the drive to achieve whatever I needed to.

Back in New Zealand, my recovery was long and slow. I celebrated my 21st birthday on the farm with my parents, the usual amount of alcohol involved, blissfully unaware of the reality of my situation. My recovery dragged on—I had damaged my spine and injured my left leg—but no one seemed too concerned, least of all me.

So, I went back to the shearing gangs, back to a life of solitude and that gnawing emptiness inside me. I tried again to get into the police force, but they put me off, saying, "You need another year without any recurring issues from your spinal injury." By the time that year passed, it was too late; I was already pregnant.

How could I be so oblivious? My loneliness and desperate need for love and acceptance had led me into a relationship with a man who was incredibly attractive to me. Not because he was a bad boy, but because he was a "real man"—tough, a bit rough, and we enjoyed drinking together.

Nothing can prepare you when you're vulnerable. Even though my parents seemed to have a respectful relationship, that wasn't something I used as a model for my own. My relationship was chaotic, built on two unhealthy people trying to have fun. We both worked hard and played hard, but when I got pregnant, I changed, and he didn't.

They say love is blind, but when you don't know what love is, you miss the basics. I thought my desperation, my need to change him, and my need for him to love me would be enough. So why did it nearly destroy me? I also had a rule for myself: I would never raise a child in a split family.

By then, life was very black and white for me. I had managed to sidestep my emotions with alcohol since I was 14. Looking back, I was a young woman, hurt and angry, wandering through life without really knowing much. Yet, some would say I thought I knew it all.

No matter what, I just kept going, because for me, there was no choice. The next 20 years of my life were like that, and even now, in many ways, life still is. Nothing comes easy for me, but more on that later.

In January 1982, my beautiful daughter came into the world. From that moment on, she was my responsibility. Her father was a man with a deeply troubled interior, though you wouldn't know it from his exterior. I guess he was a mirror reflection of me at that time. He struggled with runaway emotions and a wandering eye. He never changed when a child entered our lives, but I sure did.

Those carefree days of drinking together were over for me. I had to put on my big girl pants and do my job as a mother. The problem was, I didn't know how. Things were chaotic, filled with constant conflict. We were both desperately trying to meet our needs in unhealthy ways. There was violence, but it was the emotional and psychological abuse that did the most damage to me.

I thought I was tough enough to handle it. I thought I could change him. I knew nothing about alcoholism, drug use, or domestic violence. No way would I have considered myself a victim of domestic violence. In my mind, I could give as good as I got.

Looking back now, I see that he couldn't see his own pain. He couldn't handle those overwhelming emotions that would flare up. I believed he was a good man; I thought things could be different. But the years took their toll, and eventually, the truth of our situation broke me.

My mind goes back to those days—him working long hours, drinking every Friday, Saturday, and Sunday; me, mentally fragile and unwell, struggling with motherhood. My superwoman outfit was tattered and torn; my beauty scarred by life's harsh realities.

To me, this was normal. I'm not sure why, my Mum and Dad were not violent, I had what many would term, a 'great life as a child'. Anyway, in my young adult life I didn't question it - wasn't this how everyone lived? Our friends led similar lives—working hard, rewarding themselves with alcohol and parties at the end of the week, and the abuse just followed. No one blinked an eye; this was just how things were. I'm still not sure how I didn't know this wasn't normal. Was it because of my childhood? Because I was so deep in my own black hole that I just accepted it?

It's hard to look back and remember moments like being pushed up against a wall, 36 weeks pregnant, with a boning knife at my throat, and not thinking to run. My only thought was, *How am I going to get out of this one?* I did whatever I needed to do to not trigger a reaction that could end my life.

When I walked in the door to find the house wrecked and a .22 rifle pointed at me, I thought, *Shit, what now?*

My baby was asleep, and the babysitter was asleep too. We had been out at the pub, and when we got home, my partner was too drunk, his mind going crazy because I had taken too long to drop another guy home. I'm grateful I hid the bullets when we moved into that house. Otherwise, I'm sure I would've been dead.

It was chilling to think about my reactions that night—and his intentions. I reacted with anger; I was furious and let him know it. What the hell did he think he was doing? Turns out, he had it all planned. He had the rifle. He searched the house, turning everything upside down, trying to find the bullets. He was waiting for me, ready to shoot me when I walked through the door. Then he was going to call his sister, tell her what he'd done, and ask her to come and get the baby.

It was eerie—the plan, the intent, the cool, calm approach. Someone or something must have been watching over me that night. And yet, I still didn't leave. Life continued in the turmoil of two damaged people trying to cope with their own broken selves.

We went on to buy a house, got ourselves a truck, and tried to make a life together. It was a crazy life, and our daughter was caught up in the whirlwind of our ups and downs, exposed to all the chaos. Looking back now, I wonder how children survive such a turbulent start in life. I see now that they struggle too, just in different ways.

The violent outbursts and the heavy drinking didn't happen as often, but when they did, it felt worse—or maybe I was just less resilient. The hardest part was never knowing what version of him would walk through the door. The waiting, the uncertainty—it all wore me down. I became a nervous wreck, broken inside.

He wasn't a bad man. He was doing the best he could, given his own troubled past. But things reached a point where, every Friday night, I'd sit on the couch, too scared to lock the door because I feared he'd just kick it in. I'd sit there shaking, trembling at the thought of what was to come, determined not to provoke a fight.

It wasn't the fear of physical violence that got to me—that was almost easier to handle. He rarely hit me, and when he did, I could rationalise the pain, pick myself up, and make a mental note to dodge or duck next time. A punch was just a punch—he never beat me. Unlike other couples we knew, he never kicked me, tried to strangle me, or left me bruised and battered on the outside.

He'd come through the door, and I'd be too scared to go to bed before he got home. It wasn't just about my safety—it was about the safety of our home, too. I'd be determined not to say the wrong thing. The routine was always the same: he'd stagger in, dropped off by one of his mates, and then it would begin.

His opening words were always an invitation to battle—the topic irrelevant, designed to draw me into the fight. If I didn't take the bait, he'd argue with himself for a while, and then it would all be turned on me. I can't even remember the specifics of what he said—his words were like flaming arrows aimed at my very core. Every word was poison. Each one a blow. Inflicting pain I couldn't understand or justify. Why would he say such hurtful things?

The final straw came when I saw how it was affecting our daughter. She adored her father, and he adored her—but that wasn't enough to protect her from the chaos. When he was drunk, he couldn't tell the difference between the toilet, the wardrobe, our bedroom, or hers.

I'd lie in bed, always on high alert, ready to jump into action if he got up in the middle of the night and headed in the wrong direction. I'd try to steer him to the bathroom, but sometimes my efforts failed. There were nights when I had to pull our daughter out from under his collapsed, drunken body—his weight crushing her tiny frame.

I covered for him at work, often loading and unloading our truck by myself. I couldn't rest. I had to make sure he was awake to start his day at 2:00 a.m., depending on where his route would take him. I'd drop him off at work in the early hours because he'd lost his licence due to drunk driving, though he had a special work permit that allowed him to drive the truck, but not to get to work. One day, I noticed a girl waiting to get in the truck with him. That was the day he often had to stay over.

It was a nightmare—waiting to call the operations guy to find out if he was coming home that night or not. I felt a wave of relief when I heard he was. When I picked him up, I asked why she was with him and what would have happened if he had to stay over. He looked at me calmly and said, *"Well, she would have had to get her own room, wouldn't she?"*

The mind games, the gaslighting, it all made me feel like *I* was the one with the problem, like I was losing my grip on reality.

At the same time, my mother was dying of cancer, and I couldn't bear to let her know the truth about my life. So, I waited. I hid my pain. I held everything together as best I could, pretending everything was okay.

Waiting took its toll on me. I wasn't sure what I was waiting for—was it for things to change or for me to just disappear? Life started to feel real in a way I couldn't ignore when I realised I was too unwell to be a mother, too broken to be a partner, and barely a friend to myself.

It felt like I was living inside *The NeverEnding Story*, like the boy Bastian—a young soul tormented by bullies—finding escape in a book he stole from a dusty old bookshop. Through that book, Bastian entered Fantasia, a mythical land where he was tasked with stopping "The Nothingness", a darkness that destroyed everything in its path. The story was full of dark and depressing themes, with sad and scary moments that hit too close to home. My imagination and reason were out of balance, like the world of Fantasia itself. How could there be any balance in my life with all the chaos around me?

One scene from the film always haunted me: the moment when Atreyu's horse, Artax, sinks slowly into the Swamp of Sadness while Atreyu watches, powerless to save him. That was me—sinking into my own swamp of sadness while everyone around me watched, unable to help.

I felt powerless to change my reality, powerless to change my partner, and powerless to turn my fantasy of a better life into reality. My world was filled with "The Nothingness"—the alcohol, abuse, and endless battles. I was always trying to change something, anything, but I was stuck.

Then I reached my breaking point. I was done. No more. My anger, which had always simmered beneath the surface, finally became my motivation to change. I carried that anger like a sack of hot, burning coals—so deep and heavy that I often wondered where it all came from. But anger was also my ally—it fuelled me when nothing else could.

Anger stood at my front door, staring "The Nothingness" down. *"No more, no more, no more!"* I screamed as I threw my daughter's father's clothes onto the front lawn. It was the final full stop. **NO MORE.**

I can still feel my five-year-old daughter's grip on my leg, her desperate cries, *"Mummy, please don't throw Daddy's stuff out! Please don't!"*

But I couldn't stop. I was at my limit. *No more* was all I could say. I couldn't listen to her pleas, couldn't see her tears—this had to be done. "The Nothingness" had to be expelled from our home.

And just like that, it was over. I thought I was free—no more pain, no more alcohol, no more fear, no more conflict. But I was wrong. The hurt, the pain, the sorrow—they all remained. The need to survive remained. My all-consuming anger was still there; it just didn't have a target anymore. This moment marked the beginning of my journey beyond desperation, beyond the abuse—alone, but determined to keep going.

My life had always been a solo journey. I was used to being on my own, knowing that everything was my responsibility. I had no idea of the impact abuse and domestic violence had on me, or of the unhealthy coping strategies I'd developed just to survive. Suicide was a constant shadow in my world, but it was never an option. My daughter didn't have a father who could take responsibility; she at least deserved a mother who tried to raise her with love, who would try to help her feel good about herself and live the life she deserved.

Until that point, I had never considered that I had the power to change my life. I was blindly going through the motions, unaware of my own rights, living a life that had no value or care for myself. I didn't see myself as a victim; I didn't think I was the problem. When a doctor wrote in his report that my condition was due to my psychological state, I thought, *What the hell does that mean?* I was only aware of my physical self. Sure, my mind was a mess, but it never occurred to me that I might be psychologically unwell.

I rejected the idea of being a victim then, and I still do now. The rejection of that label came from two beliefs: my father's resilience in the face of hardship, and my own inner knowing that I would survive, no matter the demons that haunted my thoughts.

Life didn't get easier after I kicked my daughter's father out. I was still lost and alone, emotionally desperate to be loved and accepted. The black hole kept pulling me down.

By this time, I was nearly 30. My mum had died when I was 27, and though my father cared, I couldn't burden him with my troubles. My sisters didn't understand, and my brother wasn't there for me—he was too much like my daughter's father, drinking and not seeing anything wrong with it.

> ***The deep dark hole within me didn't ease;***
> ***it yearned to belong; it yearned to be loved***

Chapter Five

THE BATTLEFIELD OF SANITY

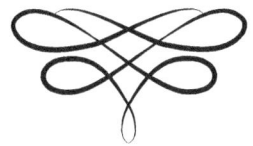

"Waging war with your demons while wearing a smile."

The next 10 years were a blur of avoiding reality. I'd slip back into my old habits now and then, drinking for a day or a night to numb the ache, but I focused on being a successful woman, mother, and employee. I lived in two worlds: one where I was alone, crying, tormented by my loneliness and the feeling that I didn't fit in, and another that I wore like a cloak whenever I stepped out into the world—the mask of *"I'm okay, nothing to see here."*

In those 10 years, I found success in the business world. I climbed ladders and earned respect, but as a mother, friend, and partner, I often fell short. I never spoke of these failures. I kept my head down, too fragile to stray from my narrow path, fearing I might shatter into a million pieces if I did.

It always felt like I was on the verge of breaking, so I did everything I could to keep it together. I battled my demons—the *"Nothingness"* that still loomed over my life—holding onto the belief that I just had to be strong. *Life's tough, and when life's tough, the tough gets going.* Even now, as I write this, I can't help but chuckle. I still don't know if my father's way of toughing things out was a blessing or a curse.

Over time, I started to understand myself a little better. I was searching for something more, aiming for better outcomes. Change didn't come easily, but it came, often pushed by necessity. My anger was still there, simmering beneath the surface, one of my most reliable tools. It was like a fire burning in my belly, protecting me, keeping others at a distance because they didn't want to face its heat.

Intimate relationships never really worked for me. The only long-term relationship I'd had was with my daughter's father, and that ended in chaos. But there was one other man who reached a deeper part of me. He was my soulmate. We were on the same journey, both searching for something to fill the emptiness inside.

We were mirrors of each other, reflecting back the same wounds, the same longings. But he accepted me for who I was. He didn't try to change me or flinch at my anger. Instead, he challenged me to think. I remember once, after I'd lashed out at him, he looked at me calmly and said, *"Rose, if anyone else had said that, you'd be laughing."*

That comment planted a seed of realisation. I saw how my overly sensitive emotions made me defensive, pushing away anything that might be good. I was trying to build a life out of dreams, but our journey was far from grounded. The space for a "well" man in my life was as distant as the stars. Wellness doesn't seek out the "unwell," and I knew that.

Being a single parent, working full-time, trying to be everything for everyone—it wasn't a recipe for success. Looking back, I probably failed miserably at most of it. I never planned to be a single mother when my daughter was just five years old, but it was the path I set us on when I finally said, *"No more."*

The ups and downs of raising a child alone took a toll on my mental health. There was no healing for me, no understanding—just sheer determination and desperation driving me forward. I lived in a constant state of turmoil, my mind and heart in chaos, longing to end it all but knowing I couldn't leave my daughter. There was only me to take responsibility, and she needed someone who cared.

There were days when the weight of living felt unbearable, like a heavy stone lodged in my chest. The thoughts of ending it all would creep in, slow at first, like a dark fog rolling in at dawn, but then they'd settle—thick and suffocating—blotting out the light. It wasn't just a fleeting notion; it became a constant whisper in the back of my mind, a steady drumbeat that I couldn't shake.

I'd lie in bed at night, staring at the ceiling, feeling the emptiness pull me under. The darkness was both a blanket and a prison, wrapping around me, offering a strange comfort in its familiarity. It would tell me that my endless tiredness, my exhaustion, would all be over—there would be no more struggling, no more injustices, no more responsibilities. The voice in my head would whisper that it was okay to let go, that the pain would finally stop.

There were moments when I felt like I was standing at the edge of a cliff, the wind howling in my ears, calling me forward. Below me, the abyss waited—a terrifying, silent invitation. The idea of falling, of surrendering to that void, was almost beautiful. It promised an end to the turmoil, to the never-ending battles inside my head. It promised peace—the kind of peace I hadn't felt in years.

I'd think about the act itself, the mechanics of it, and there was a cold, clinical detachment in those thoughts. A plan would form—logical and precise—as if I were solving a problem. I imagined the relief that might wash over me in that final moment: the release, the escape, the silence. I imagined a world where I didn't have to fight so hard just to get through the day.

But then, like a flicker in the dark, a sliver of something would break through—a slight strength would rise from deep within, and I would somehow climb out of the depths of despair and keep going. For a moment, the fog would lift just enough for me to take my next breath. The drumbeat would fade in the light of another day, and the threads of responsibility anchoring me to this world would again take control.

The battle has never really been over—just pushed to the background, waiting. But in those moments, I chose to stay. For others. I chose to face another day, to fight another fight, because maybe, just maybe, one day I would wake with a renewed zest for life—moments of enjoyment, and freedom from the torment of the demons.

Knowing what it's like to fight your desire for death creates a level of empathy for others that reflects an understanding beyond words. There's no need for panic. There's no need to say anything. There's just acceptance—and connection—in the silence.

I feel things deeply—deep sadness and pain. Over those years, it was as if someone had switched something off inside me. I was here, but not really. I went through the motions of living, but it felt like I was watching someone else play out my life on a screen. I'd smile when I was supposed to smile, say the right things when I was supposed to speak—but it all felt hollow, like an echo in an empty room.

There was a numbness that settled into my bones—an emptiness I couldn't shake. It was as if my soul had been stripped away, leaving just the shell of a person behind. I would wake up each day and go through the routine—brush my teeth, get dressed, go to work—but I didn't feel connected to any of it. I was like a puppet, moving only because the strings were being pulled.

Sometimes I'd catch a glimpse of myself in the mirror, and I wouldn't recognise the person staring back. The eyes looked the same, but there was no light in them—no spark. Just two blank orbs reflecting a face that seemed so familiar, yet so foreign to me. I'd search for something familiar in those eyes, some sign that I was still in there somewhere, but all I saw was a void staring back at me.

Conversations felt like a chore—each word heavy and deliberate, as though I were reading lines from a script. I'd nod and laugh when I should, but inside, there was nothing. No genuine feeling. No warmth. Just a cold, vast emptiness. It was as if all the colours in my life had faded, leaving everything in shades of grey.

I tried to fill the emptiness inside me with distractions—burying myself in work, losing hours to television, throwing everything into my career. My phone became my constant companion, always there to numb the silence, always giving me something to do, something to focus on. I made choices I thought were best, but in doing so, I created distance between my daughter and me—a chasm shaped by my own emptiness. I often wondered what it would feel like to truly enjoy life, to have the kind of connection with my daughter that I imagined other mothers had with theirs.

I achieved things that many never get the chance to. On paper, my life looked like a success. But inside, I remained cold, detached, untouched by any sense of accomplishment. Yet, I found myself drawn to others who were broken in their own ways—those who carried their own heavy burdens. My place seemed to be with them, with those who had faced the worst life could throw at them.

And somehow, from within that shared darkness, a light began to flicker. A small, almost imperceptible spark of hope that tempted me towards something more. It was as if, through their struggles, I began to see a path for myself—a calling that could give my life the meaning it had been missing.

I walked away from the corporate world, thinking I was leaving the battlefield behind. I believed that stepping into a career in social services would be different—that people would be more open and willing to work together towards positive outcomes. I imagined a place where the focus wasn't on conflict or competition, but on creating real, meaningful change—something beneficial for everyone involved. I thought I was entering a world where people cared more about lifting each other up than tearing each other down.

> **Decades later, I walked away from my home, my country, and the pain. The first thing I experienced was I found someone genuine, kind, and caring to share life with. That was a gift that has allowed me to be me, and write this story.**

PART TWO

WHAT DOESN'T WORK AND WHY

Are we truly living the Australian dream, or merely wandering through a haze of smoke and mirrors, whispering comforting tales to ourselves as the very foundations crack beneath our feet?

Bathed in the glow of optimism, we claim to be addressing the wicked social issues that plague our communities. But peer beneath the surface—really look—and what do you see? A landscape littered with unmet promises, where the true stories tell of failure far more often than success.

I used to believe in the collective strength of common sense—that if we could all simply see the truth, we could fix what was broken. But time and again, I've raised the flag: *This isn't working.* We're not creating the impact we claim to be, and time and again, I've been told, *"You don't see the full picture."*

But perhaps the problem is that I see it all too clearly.

I'm not alone in this. Others see it too, but too few of us are still standing, still fighting to shift the grim realities that have loomed large for over two decades.

The Australian Bureau of Statistics dutifully compiles the numbers, laying them out in neat rows and columns. With those figures, we can craft almost any narrative we choose. But step back—let your eyes unfocus just a little—and the picture becomes far less comforting. Let me show you what I see when I trace these facts.

In **2004**, around **one in five Australians** was living with a **mental health disorder** (ABS, 2008). For young people aged 16–24, nearly **19% experienced psychological distress** (AIHW, 2005). The **suicide rate** stood at **10.4 per 100,000 lives**. And yet—only a **third of those struggling reached out for help** (Department of Health, 2023).

By **2014**, the needle had barely moved. Still one in five Australians faced mental illness. But **anxiety** had tightened its grip, and **youth distress climbed higher**. Suicide crept up to **12 per 100,000** (AIHW, 2015). Programmes like **Better Access** had widened the doorway to care—**46%** of people were now accessing support. Yet despite more help, more funding, more awareness… the suffering remained as relentless as ever.

And now, here we are in **2024**, standing in the echo of all those efforts—surrounded by well-meaning policies and expensive frameworks that still fail to deliver **real change**. One in five Australians continues to grapple with mental health challenges (ABS, 2024). But the battles have deepened. They're now **entangled with trauma, addiction, disconnection**, and a rising tide of hopelessness.

Among young people, **psychological distress has soared to nearly 25%**—driven by the fears of our age: climate anxiety, digital overload, pandemic echoes (Mission Australia & Black Dog Institute, 2024). **Suicide rates remain heartbreakingly high**, especially in **rural and Indigenous communities** (ABS, 2024). Yes, over **half of those in need now seek help**, aided by **digital platforms and telehealth**—but the pain lingers. The tide has not turned.

And what of the money?

Since 2003, **mental health funding has ballooned**—from modest billions to **$6.3 billion in 2023** (Commonwealth of Australia, 2023). But the return on that investment? Statistically flat. **Still one in five. Still the same silent struggles.** The system spins narratives to explain away its inertia, but the reality is simple and sobering: after **two decades**, the suffering remains **largely unchanged**.

Then there's **alcohol**—another shadow across our national psyche. In 2004, **13% of Australians drank at risky levels** (AIHW, 2005). By 2014, that figure rose to **18%**, and hospital admissions followed (AIHW, 2015). In 2024, **31% of Australians aged 14+ drink at dangerous levels** (AIHW, 2024). Fewer teens may be sneaking a first sip underage—but more adults are **drowning in habits they can't seem to escape**.

And drugs? The numbers are slippery—**hidden behind stigma and illegality**. But they whisper enough. **The problem isn't going away** (AIHW, 2023). If anything, it's evolving.

Meanwhile, the broader social landscape groans under the weight of **domestic violence, elder abuse, youth crime**—issues that continue their quiet march, unfazed by initiatives that never quite touch the root (ABS, 2023; AIHW, 2022).

We have **the numbers. We have the resources. We have the language.**
And yet, what we don't seem to have—still—is real change.

And so, we come to the next chapter of this story—one written in sorrow, frustration, and hard-won truth. The systems we depend on are broken. The services we turn to are failing. And no one is being held accountable.

How long can we support a system that's not only failing to solve our problems, but is collapsing under its own denial?

How long can we keep pretending we're "onto it" when the evidence screams we're drowning in it?

Chapter One

THE SYSTEM

"Built to help. Structured to fail."

Here we go again—another story of blame, another tale of evading responsibility.

It might sound like I'm talking about a client or a family member, but honestly, this is me wrestling with my own thoughts and feelings. My head was trying to make sense of it all, while my heart ached, caught in the clash between my long-held beliefs and the brutal reality of the 'system' I had just stepped into.

Leaving the corporate world behind, I entered the social services field with high hopes. I thought I was swapping the cutthroat grind of performance reviews and profit margins for a space shaped by compassion, where the goal was to uplift, not compete. I imagined a world where my passion for helping others could finally take root and thrive—where my life experiences could be transformed into meaningful change.

But the reality hit hard.

I had walked in armed with the frameworks and expectations from my corporate background, assuming they would serve me well in this new journey. I was wrong.

My first taste of the social services world was a jolt. As an intern, I encountered a reality far removed from the supportive, collaborative environment I had envisioned. Instead of the fulfilling work I had dreamed of, I faced resistance, disillusionment, and systemic dysfunction. The very dynamics I had hoped to escape—conflict, rigid hierarchies, emotional burnout—were all present, just wearing different uniforms.

My decision to leave the corporate battlefield had been driven by a yearning for something more—something real. But what I encountered wasn't just a career shift. It was a reckoning with my own expectations. It was a plunge into a system whose struggles were buried deep in its bones.

My life experiences had fuelled a fierce determination. I believed that surely this work—this service to others—would be more rewarding than the constant grind of corporate life, where I'd repeatedly slammed into the invisible ceiling of a male-dominated space. I was no longer chasing the dollar. I was chasing purpose.

Yes, I had a gift for generating income for organisations, but the lack of recognition, the politics, and the unrelenting conflict chipped away at me until I could no longer pretend it was sustainable. I made a life-altering choice: I had to step away.

The System

In 1999, I walked through the doors of a well-known government organisation, ready to begin my new role as an alcohol and drug counsellor intern. I had juggled full-time study and the relentless need to bring in a wage since parenthood, but I arrived fuelled by sheer determination—a need to belong, and a vision for a better future.

On day one, I turned up in my familiar black 'corporate' trousers and a neat, smart-casual top, my heart brimming with optimism. I made my way to the manager's office, hoping to become a valued part of the team. I imagine most people start in this field with the same spark, but now I know few manage to keep it alight. The system wears people down—thread by thread—until their tether to humanity is left frayed and torn.

I was fully aware that I was the new kid on the block. I had no formal knowledge of mental health or addiction—only what I had lived. My enthusiasm, endless questions, and hunger to learn were, at times, met with visible distaste, especially from those in senior roles. It didn't take long before I realised—yet again—I didn't quite fit.

Still, I hurled myself into the work. There was something in me, a zest for humanity, that got me out of bed with purpose each morning. My first few days were filled with a lightness in my step. I was ready to support and grow. A handful of clinicians welcomed my energy and shared my drive for real change. But many, especially those in positions of authority, did not.

They didn't just reject me. They rejected my desire to empower others. They dismissed my hope that we could do better.

All the dreams I'd carried—my ambitions, my ideals—stalled. I had stepped into a world that looked nothing like I'd imagined. And not in a good way.

This community-based government agency was a maze of bureaucracy. The air was thick with detachment. The culture wasn't one of care or compassion, but one where clients were too often seen as case files and metrics—commodities rather than human beings.

It didn't take long, however, before I realised that—once again—I was the odd one out.

What struck me most wasn't just the sense of not belonging. It was the startling absence of accountability. No one seemed truly responsible for their actions or the outcomes they produced. Subpar results weren't just tolerated—they were normalised. Or perhaps it was something more insidious: a system that nurtured and protected the title of 'professional' so tightly, so fervently, that no one dared to question the system itself.

And that's exactly what *'it'* was.

'It' was the system I would come to know across many government departments and social service organisations—rigid, self-preserving, and quietly hostile to any challenge, even when that challenge was simply an honest question.

I stood in an office surrounded by so-called experts, their voices droning on as they told me how *I* needed to change. Their words echoed, but they barely registered. My heart ached. My head spun. And slowly, a bitter truth began to crystallise.

Broken Families, Broken Systems, Broken Promises
The System

I didn't yet have the language for what I was feeling, but I now know that moment sparked something fierce within me—a kind of ignition. A bone-deep sense of injustice. That feeling would become a recurring theme throughout my journey. A relentless pulse urging me to try and make things right.

I hadn't expected to find such injustice here, in this field that was meant to care. But there it was, staring back at me with indifference.

It was in this cold and clinical world that I met Sarah. Her story would etch itself into my memory and never quite leave.

She was just 18 years old, though she'd already endured more than most would in a lifetime. Her life was stitched together with threads of neglect, betrayal, and abuse—woven by the very people who were meant to love and protect her. Sarah had recently transitioned from child and adolescent mental health services into the adult system. There was no proper handover. No warm introduction. Just a file, a broken soul, and me—an intern, given the responsibility of being her new case manager.

From the very beginning, I leaned into what I knew best: connection, rapport, and the kind of language that didn't just communicate but comforted. Sarah was different. She saw through the walls that people usually put up. She sensed I genuinely cared. And slowly, she began to trust me.

She told me, more than once, "You're not like the others."

Sarah's world was shaped by confusion and isolation. I had never encountered someone so utterly lost, so haunted by her own mind. She desperately craved connection. She was reaching for something solid, something kind, in a world that had only ever shown her pain.

Her early years had been a kind of imprisonment. A cage of trauma that had stunted her emotional and psychological development. Sometimes, her behaviour mirrored that of a much younger child—a defence mechanism shaped by years of survival.

In Sarah, I didn't just see a client, I saw a human being crying out to be seen, to be heard, to be held in a world that kept turning away. She remains with me to this day. A quiet reminder of why I do what I do. A whisper in my heart that says: *This is why you must keep going.*

Sarah was strikingly beautiful. Her long ash-blonde hair flowed like a silken stream, her slight frame an unintended siren's call, but what should have been a blessing became a cruel curse. Men treated her with cold indifference or unmasked desire—each interaction a new echo of the abuse she had known all her life.

In the corridors of mental health buildings, among the professionals who should have been her protectors, I saw it again: the same disregard. The same coldness. Her trauma and beauty ignored or exploited; her suffering tucked away beneath the daily paperwork.

Her existence swung between fleeting moments of lucidity and crashing waves of chaos. She reminded me of a time not so long ago when people like her would have been locked away in institutions, labelled and forgotten.

Sarah wasn't beyond redemption. She wasn't broken. She was abandoned by a society too tired or too frightened to care properly.

And as I walked further into the machinery of the system, I could feel my own values, my own sense of purpose, beginning to shrink under the weight of it all. The tide of indifference was constant, and no matter how hard I tried, I could feel my spirit beginning to erode.

I had hoped I could change things from the inside. I had tried to hold on. But it became clear—I couldn't do it alone.

After just a few months, I knew it was time. I left that role and accepted a new position as clinical manager of the drug treatment unit in what was then New Zealand's largest men's prison.

Leaving Sarah behind was a bittersweet necessity.

Our final meeting unfolded in one of those stark, institutional rooms—locked away from the world outside. It was a space where Sarah had dared to trust me, where she had revealed fragile glimpses of her soul. But that day, our farewell became a haunting moment that still lingers in my memory.

When Sarah heard I was leaving, her reaction was visceral—terror-stricken, like a deer caught in the glare of headlights. Her instincts ricocheted between flight, fight, or freeze. In the end, she froze. With a trembling hug and sorrowful eyes, she offered a hesitant goodbye. We exchanged a tearful, "See you later," though deep down, we both knew there might never be another meeting.

As she walked away, I expected her to exit the building, but she didn't. Instead, she lingered in the shadowed corridor before quietly slipping into another room and locking the door behind her.

A growing unease crept in. The atmosphere shifted. I was soon alerted to Sarah's presence behind that locked door, and panic spread. My colleagues scrambled to respond, their voices edged with fear, afraid she might harm herself. The master key was summoned. And finally, with a reluctant twist, the door creaked open.

The room was cloaked in shadow. In the far corner, Sarah lay curled in a foetal position. The floor was damp beneath her, the soaked carpet silently bearing witness to her distress. She was unresponsive—still, withdrawn, unreachable. Her silence roared louder than any scream.

I stood, frozen, struck by helplessness. I reached out to more experienced colleagues, pleading for support—if not for answers, then at least for dignity. I phoned the acute mental health crisis team. Their office was just down the street, but they refused to come, dismissing the urgency of her state.

Frustrated and heartsick, I turned to my manager. The response was ice-cold: if Sarah hadn't left the building by the end of the day, I was to call the police to have her removed.

My stomach twisted into knots.
How could anyone suggest this as an acceptable response? The idea of leaving her in such a state—without compassion, without care—felt like a fist to my chest.

Time ticked on. The pool on the carpet grew larger, a silent symbol of a girl lost in trauma. The hour approached. My options evaporated.

With a heavy heart, I made the call.

It felt like a betrayal. A surrender. A soul-crushing moment in which hope slipped quietly away.

My final image of Sarah is seared into my mind: four policemen—two gripping her arms, two her legs—carrying her limp body down the hallway. A female officer followed, her face unreadable. I trailed behind, numb, as the procession moved outside. A bitter wind sliced through the late afternoon.

On the street, they laid her on the cold tarmac behind the van.

The door opened. Her body, still unresponsive, was lifted and dragged into the back of the van, onto its cold, stainless steel floor. That sterile metal was a far cry from the warmth and humanity she so desperately needed.

As the vehicle pulled away, I stood there, shaken, staring down the road. I knew where she was going. I could see it in my mind: concrete walls, flickering fluorescent lights, the void of a police cell—and the distant, locked mental health room that awaited her.

I'll never understand how anyone could justify such demeaning disregard for another human being.

Sarah remained in that catatonic state for two long weeks before she began to emerge.

The last I heard, she was in a relationship and had a child. I can only hope that somewhere in our brief connection, she found a small ember of strength to carry her through. I hope she found more than survival—I hope she found a path forward.

Throughout my career, I never met a person who was truly "bad." Every soul I encountered was a reflection of compassion, wounded and worn by life's storms. Sarah was no exception. Amid all her suffering, she gifted me something unforgettable—a poem.

Her words, delicate and raw, were a mirror into her world. They carved through the silence, exposing her inner torment with breathtaking honesty. That poem wasn't just a reflection of her pain—it was her soul, handwritten and shared. It remains tucked inside me, a part of her that still whispers across time.

Her Poem

Their faces are haggard before their time
I don't want that face for mine
I am happy with my own mask
One sane day is all I ask

The bottle won't let go –
Not the hand upon its neck
The holder once was sober
Now she's just a wreck

Once she liked to party
Now she drinks alone
Gone beyond being social
She hides and skulls at home

They share a comfortable silence
Often found with friends
Sitting there, the drink, the drunk
To their separate ends

I see them there together
And shudder as I think
I recognise those faces
It is me and my drink

Sarah's story is not simply a tragedy—it's an exposé.

It lays bare the failures not of the people, but of the system itself. It reveals machinery built on detachment and indifference.

Her journey—and so many others like it—pulls back the curtain on a world that speaks of care but too often forgets how to *care*. A world that overlooks the wounded. A world that measures success in numbers, not lives.

In the end, it doesn't matter whether you're a client, a family member, or a clinician.

The system chews through you just the same.

It drains your hope. It swallows your strength. And it lets you walk out the door without a shred of 'caring' left in you.

A system proud of its key performance indicators (KPIs), counting numbers through the door and tallying minutes spent with each case, but it forgets what really matters— human beings, crying out to be seen.

Chapter Two

IVORY TOWERS AND PEDESTALS

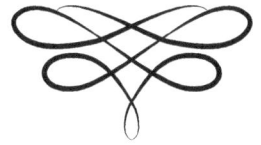

"When those who hold the power forget those who need the care."

In the bustling, labyrinthine heart of our modern world lies a chasm—an ever-expanding gulf between the lofty ideals of compassion and the stark realities faced by those seeking support from addiction services, mental health services, justice, and youth services.

Picture a realm where hearts are set on noble intentions, yet the methods employed miss the mark by a mile. As the carousel of assistance spins, failing time and again to deliver lasting change, who pauses to ask: ***Are we unintentionally nurturing the very failure we seek to overcome?***

In this fractured landscape, the pursuit of transformation often stumbles over its own inadequacies. The question of whether our approaches are fuelling the very patterns we claim to fight remains unspoken, leaving a void where genuine progress could take root.

Stepping out of the corporate world and into the domain of social services, I embarked on a journey of profound revelation. The corporate corridors I had left behind—where success hinged on the dance of KPIs, ticking boxes, and collecting pay cheques—stood in stark contrast to the ideal I'd imagined of the social services world.

I had expected a different kind of accountability—one where numbers reflected not just bureaucratic compliance but real, tangible impact on human lives.

Instead of the vibrant, evidence-based transformation I had envisioned, I found myself caught in the mundane machinery of quotas and spreadsheets. What I hoped would be a beacon of meaningful progress turned out to be little more than an illusion. A mirage, carefully constructed with terms like "outcomes" and "deliverables," yet ultimately disconnected from the lived experience of those it claimed to serve.

How, I wondered, does counting the number of people seen in a day truly reflect a *return on investment*, if the investment was supposed to be change, and not just service provision?

In this new world, where the stakes are nothing short of life and death, and the need for profound change is as real as the ground beneath our feet, the shadow of true accountability remained elusive. It felt as though the sun and moon danced in their celestial rhythms, never touching, forever separated by a chasm of unfulfilled promises. The transformation I had so deeply longed for seemed as distant as the stars themselves.

Across every organisation I encountered in both New Zealand and Australia, the pursuit of accountability seemed to vanish into thin air. It was replaced by an endless game of smoke and mirrors.

"Evidence-based practice" was paraded as the gold standard—not a guiding star, but a brilliant distraction. A mantra chanted so often and so confidently, it lulled us into a dangerous sleep. It obscured the need for real reflection, the kind that might force us to confront the truth of our own ineffectiveness.

In the quiet corners of my mind, the phrase echoes still. "Evidence-based practice." But what evidence are we really clinging to? What metrics justify the millions poured into services that remain unable—or unwilling—to evolve?

Many of these services, perched atop their self-appointed pedestals, believe they hold the answers. They project certainty, expertise, and authority. But when you step into the homes and lives of those they claim to help, a different story emerges. The silence is deafening.

Not one person sings the praises of these systems. Not a client. Not a mother. Not a partner. And yet, we all persist in believing—*the professionals will help. The professionals must help.*

It's as though an unspoken pact exists between providers and funders: pour more money in, and something good will eventually spill out. It's a comforting fantasy. But the reality on the ground is stark.

Despite the rhetoric, poverty deepens. Addiction festers. Mental health crises multiply.

In the vast expanse of social services, mental health, and justice, evidence should illuminate the way forward. But what happens when that light begins to flicker? When it fades, and all we're left with is a dim glow of good intentions? The truth becomes harder to ignore: *our best efforts are falling short.*

There's a fundamental disconnect between our belief that services can resolve these wicked problems and the complex, tangled nature of human lives. So, we must ask—*what's the true purpose of these services?* Stripped of jargon, unwrapped from layers of justification and funding rationale, what are they really meant to do? And how well are they doing it? Some offer support. Many mean well. But few ignite the kind of real, lasting transformation they promise.

Through my years in the field, I've come to understand that people aren't inherently broken. I've worked alongside brilliant professionals, filled with compassion and hope, but I've also seen the dangers of rigid thinking.

A mind closed to new perspectives soon becomes a heart closed to new possibilities.
The system itself—fragmented, inflexible, and fiercely protective of its silos—breeds this stagnation.

Each specialised service clings to its corner, offering partial solutions and patchwork remedies. Meanwhile, precious public funds are siphoned into endless reform efforts that lack cohesion and vision.

The result? Surface-level fixes. No integration. No holistic view of the person.

Imagine someone in crisis, stepping into the system, desperate for help.

They're met not with clarity, but with a maze. One path leads to a trauma psychologist. Another to an addiction specialist. Down another hall awaits a behavioural change expert. And just around the corner, someone suggests perhaps a sexual assault counsellor should be added too.

And so begins the circuit. The appointments. The assessments. The retelling of trauma—again and again. The fragmentation is overwhelming. The system, meant to heal, becomes another layer of harm.

This intricate web of referrals forms a fragmented mosaic of care—a maze where those seeking help are confronted with long waitlists, complex intake screenings, and multiple assessments. And if, by some miracle, they return after this exhausting process, they're handed not one clear solution but a stack of disconnected treatment plans.

Services too often operate in a way that reflects bureaucratic necessity rather than human need. Funding is utilised to satisfy reporting requirements, not to create meaningful engagement. The very design of the system eliminates the opportunity for genuine connection, for real support in resolving the issues at hand.

The ever-expanding waitlists and elusive appointment slots pile on layers of frustration, hopelessness, and despair. The evidence is there for all to see: the network built to offer aid is buckling beneath the weight of human suffering.

The time has come to stop blindly chasing failed strategies. We need a u-turn—a shift rooted in humility, guided by courage, and powered by an open mind.

We must acknowledge the disconnection. It stretches not just between services, but between professionals from different domains. So many voices, so little true cooperation. In my experience, "collaboration" too often means exchanging polite emails, not actually walking beside one another to support the individual and their family.

I remember reaching out to a mental health case worker, hoping to work in partnership on behalf of a client. I sent a respectful email introducing myself, only to receive a reply that stunned me:

> **"The mother is the primary problem.
> She's the reason the client is unwell."**

No, I screamed deep within!

The client has a diagnosable mental health condition—treatment-resistant schizophrenia. The mother wasn't the problem. She may have been lost, unsure, terrified, and desperate for guidance, but she wasn't to blame. She was simply a woman relying on the mental health system to carve out a path to recovery.

Youth justice offers another vivid example of a system attempting to protect its streets while failing to reach the hearts of those caught in chaos. Locking young people away may silence the immediate threat, but it does nothing to heal the root causes of their behaviour.

Throughout my career, I've worked with many of these young people—lost boys and girls spinning in their own storms, their households flipped upside down, their parents rendered powerless.

So, let's ask the question: at what age can a child genuinely make wise, life-altering decisions?

During a brief period in youth residential care, I witnessed a system that had lost its way. The dominant philosophy was permissive parenting—an approach that, from the outset, seemed destined to fail.

Rules were rarely enforced. Boundaries were fluid. Consequences came only when the situation escalated to crisis levels, usually involving police intervention. The chaos became a cycle.

Let me be clear: I don't support youth detention as a first response, but when no other effective alternatives exist, it can sometimes be the lesser evil.

Take one young man I encountered. His history read like a tragic novel—repeated offences, multiple youth justice orders, endless stints in detention. And still, nothing changed.

When he was triggered, destruction followed. He broke over 10 televisions, smashed a staff member's car, and left entire rooms in ruins—windows shattered, fridges overturned, food thrown like paint across floors and walls.

It was carnage.

The staff tried to calm him, to de-escalate the storm, but their efforts rarely worked.

To staff one of these residential homes, a Certificate IV in youth work (CHC40413) was required, alongside some hands-on experience. But many workers were there because they needed a job, not because they understood the complexities of behaviour change.

Tick the boxes. Meet the quota. Fear the funding cuts. That's what drove the system.

And sadly, the same could be said for some of the managers—well-meaning, perhaps, but unaware of what real behaviour management entails.

Over the years, my connection with young people has taught me one undeniable truth:

You cannot change behaviour without first earning respect.
And respect doesn't mean permissiveness.
It doesn't mean being their friend.

Respect means boundaries.
Respect means consistency.
Respect means following through—every time.

We must lead by example. Expectations shouldn't be whispered; they should be *modelled*, *reinforced*, and *lived*.

I remember that boy—the one who left nothing unbroken. Before he was placed in the house, he warned everyone: *"If you put me there, I'll destroy it."*

And true to his word, he did.

He wasn't manipulative. He wasn't trying to be cruel. He was telling the truth—the only way he knew how.

When I reported the destruction to the manager, their immediate response was to replace the ruined items. I stood firm. I refused to buy new furniture or any non-essential items.

My reasoning was simple: this young man needed a safe environment, not a reinforced cycle. Replacing the damage without consequence would only validate the behaviour that caused it. Instead, we cleared the debris and restored the basics—his bed, food, and physical safety. The rest would remain untouched.

The manager's primary concern? Child Safety might visit and question why the house appeared unfurnished.

But the real issue they had was with what they labelled *restrictive practice*.

In their eyes, withholding furniture fell into that category. In mine, it was *harm reduction*. By not restocking the house with objects he could destroy, I was reducing the likelihood of further incidents and the inevitable police charges that would follow. Arrests were a regular part of this young man's life.

To me, restrictive practice involves direct control—physical restraint, seclusion, forced isolation. This wasn't that. This was consequence without condemnation. It was a choice grounded in respect: acknowledging his autonomy while also making clear that actions have outcomes. He didn't need an explanation. He understood.

After yet another behavioural outburst and a short return to youth detention, he was placed in a new home—this time, further from the watchful eyes of neighbours. I made sure this new environment was intentionally minimal. Anything that could be used as a weapon was removed. The pantry held only the essentials. Non-essentials were stored securely. His room was furnished with care—only what was needed, and only with items I knew he wouldn't destroy because they now belonged to *him*.

Why take such a hard line?

Because I had seen the fury. I had witnessed the projectiles launched at staff—the cans, the glass, the chaos. A single thrown object could do permanent damage.

So I acted not from fear, but from responsibility. This wasn't punishment, it was protection. For him. For the staff. For the possibility of something better.

When he returned to this stripped-back environment, he didn't protest. He didn't need to. He *understood*.

He may have resented me, but he adapted.

I've always believed my role isn't to be a friend, but a protector.

Safety is the foundation. Respect is a constant. And predictability—through consistent consequences, clear boundaries, and realistic expectations—builds trust.

When intentions are clear and respect is mutual, growth becomes possible. That's when you plant the seeds for independence, self-efficacy, and something stronger than survival.

Early in his second week back, he approached me with a request:

"Can I have a TV in the lounge again?"

"And can the food go back in the pantry and fridge?"

My answer was simple: "Sure. No problem."

I didn't demand promises or threats of consequences. I didn't need conditions. I trusted that he now understood the boundaries. And I knew if things went wrong again, we'd respond with the same calm, consistent, harm-reducing approach.

What so often fails in youth work—and more broadly, in social services—is the mistaken belief that *being a friend* will solve the problem.

But these young people don't need friends.

They need *support*.

They need *structure*.

They need to know that respect and natural consequences go hand-in-hand.

The gap in training across these services is glaring. Workers arrive with hearts in the right place, but little understanding of behaviour change. Systems are stretched thin—demand is high, resources are few, and the ivory tower mentality remains intact.

My question is, and always has been:

What's realistic? And what support does this person need to be the best they can be—*right now*?

During my time overseeing youth in residential care, it became painfully clear: young people were being set up to fail.

The core issue wasn't the behaviour—it was the lack of consequences. It was a workforce that didn't understand the mechanics of change.

The outbursts, the destruction, the running away—they were all forms of expression. These young people were screaming through their behaviour. And that's okay. They didn't know any other way.

For many, it became a game. A game to control an environment that lacked structure. A game without rules or referees.

When staff try to *be friends*, it backfires.

A child runs. Staff chase them. The child runs again. Staff chase harder. And so the game continues—*catch me if you can.*

And no prizes for guessing who wins.

These kids know about fear. They can sniff it. And when they sense uncertainty, they exploit it—not out of cruelty, but because it's *effective*. If it gets them out of trouble or lets them dodge accountability, they'll use it.

Another issue? *Splitting.*

Inexperienced staff are vulnerable to it. They think a child favouring them means they're doing well. But in truth, it often signals inconsistency.

A staff team that isn't aligned becomes a breeding ground for chaos.

In my time managing residential care, I saw little evidence of a united front. Managers played favourites. They criticised staff in front of others. And worst of all, they enabled the very behaviours they were meant to address.

A disliked staff member was assumed to be ineffective.

But in reality?

The more pushback I received from residents wasn't because I was failing. It was because I *couldn't be manipulated. I wouldn't be split.*

And they knew it.

Young people in care aren't required to attend school. They're not held to their court-ordered courses. If they choose not to take their medication, that's acceptable too. They come and go from their residential placements as they please—no consequence, no accountability. Substance use is commonplace. Disruptive behaviour isn't just tolerated, it's expected.

I'm reminded of this new wave of thinking that has swept through the sector—a mindset where responsibility has all but vanished, replaced by the belief that it's a child's 'right' to have complete autonomy over their lives.

And I find myself dumbfounded.

How can well-educated, experienced adults truly believe that a child—especially one who has never had a stable foundation, never been taught responsibility, nor equipped with the tools to solve problems—can make consistently informed decisions about their own wellbeing?

We label these children as 'bad' and then do nothing to help them understand who they are or what they could become.

Meanwhile, professionals—ensconced in their glass towers—remain convinced that their programmes are working. That their efforts are enough.

I was starkly reminded of this delusion when the young man I spoke of earlier stood before a judge once again, facing fresh charges of property damage. The court was considering returning him to detention, but his legal representatives fought against it.

Youth justice stepped in, assuring the judge: "We have community programmes to support this young man."

The judge, wise and weary, peered over the rim of his glasses and responded without hesitation: "Well, looking at how many programmes this young man has previously been sentenced to—and his extensive criminal history—I'm inclined to think they haven't worked for him."

There are gaping holes in the system.

Throughout my time overseeing his residential placement, not once was I formally consulted about his presentation or behaviour.

Not by youth justice.

Not by his legal team.

Not by mental health.

It struck me as absurd. I was the one with the most direct oversight, the one witnessing his daily triumphs and his darkest spirals. Yet my insights were never sought.

Staff were driven by mantras:

"The police are the last resort."

"Detention is a failure of the system."

"The mother is to blame."

I disagreed with all of it.

I valued the relationship with the police. I supported them in supporting these young people. Communication was key. But the ivory tower mentality prevailed—those at the top assumed they understood what was happening on the ground, while rarely setting foot there.

This belief that "the experts know best"—that one professional will ride in on a white horse and vanquish all the challenges of community dysfunction—isn't just unrealistic, it's dangerous.

No single person, no single service, can carry the weight of this crisis alone.

And if those who claim to know best *truly did*, then surely by now we would be seeing progress—*real, measurable progress*.

We wouldn't still be watching the same patterns play out in our schools, homes, courts, and streets.

Instead, we witness the same revolving door: of families pleading for support, of young people stuck in chaos, of overworked professionals repeating interventions that don't work—because they must, not because they believe in them.

The system fails.

Professionals look away.

Funders cling to comfortable illusions.

But the truth stands firm: *not much is changing.*

There's an ongoing question—echoing through corridors and across boardroom tables—about whether professionals working inside a dysfunctional system can ever truly influence meaningful change.

> *If we cannot reduce demand...*
> *If we cannot shift outcomes...*
> *If we cannot empower the people we serve...*
> *Then what, exactly, are we doing?*

Chapter Three

THE DESTRUCTION OF CULTURE

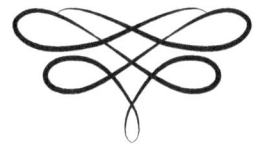

"When we lose our roots, we lose our way."

Imagine a grand tapestry, woven with intricate threads of customs, beliefs, and practices. Traditional culture is the loom on which this tapestry rests—a dynamic framework that has long sustained communities, preserving their identity while gracefully adapting through time.

Now, picture a hidden valley, where the golden sun kisses ancient stones and the breeze carries the songs of old. In this sacred place, traditional culture breathes—not as a relic of the past, but as a vibrant force pulsing through daily life.

Here, each dawn is greeted with the soft chant of morning rituals. Each sunset is honoured by communal gatherings, storytelling, and gratitude. This world isn't hurried or disconnected. It's rhythmically alive, its heartbeat syncing with the land, the sky, and the whispered wisdom of ancestors.

At the heart of it all is reverence for those who came before. The ancestors aren't merely remembered, but honoured as active guides, their spirits believed to live within the trees, the rivers, and the very breath of the people. Their wisdom echoes in the wind, in story, in ceremony.

Social organisation flows like an elegant dance—each role purposeful, each relationship defined by respect and tradition. Elders, adorned not in wealth but in experience, are the compass points. Their stories shape the future. Their counsel maintains the balance.

Ceremonies aren't performances, but sacred acts of connection, rites of passage marking life's transitions, seasonal festivals attuned to nature's cycles. They bind generations, past and present, in colourful expression and ritual memory.

Customary laws and norms form the invisible threads of community life. Though unwritten, they're understood, woven into every interaction and resolution. They maintain harmony, not through punishment, but through shared values, accountability, and trust.

Traditional knowledge isn't archived in books but is lived. Passed from hand to hand, voice to voice, it resides in woven cloth, medicinal herbs, carved symbols, and oral histories. It's not static, it evolves yet remains rooted in the wisdom of those who came before.

Language is melody. Art is ceremony. Expression is identity. Through songs, rhythms, sculptures, and symbols, culture is kept alive, animated by the energy of collective memory.

Broken Families, Broken Systems, Broken Promises
The Destruction of Culture

Education in this world isn't standardised or siloed—it's embodied. Children learn through observation, participation, and stories told beneath starlit skies. They're shaped not by classrooms, but by community.

And economy is no less sacred. Hunting, farming, gathering—these acts of subsistence are ceremonies of gratitude. To take from the Earth is to honour it. Every harvest is both sustenance and prayer.

In this living symphony, traditional culture is the instrument of connection between people, land, and spirit. A dynamic harmony that sings of belonging.

But now, the melody is fading.

In the grand theatre of society—where once the curtains of tradition stood firm, where community values held the stage—a dramatic shift has taken place.

The spotlight has turned.

Where once there was collective harmony, now there's individual triumph. The pursuit of power and control has replaced the pursuit of unity. The hunger is insatiable—a gluttonous grasp for dominance that gnaws at the threads of cultural cohesion.

And as the cultural fabric begins to fray, it's like watching a magnificent tapestry unravel one thread at a time. One belief. One role. One ritual. Gone.

What was once a grand mosaic—each tile held in place by shared values—now shatters under the weight of modern disconnection. Pieces scatter. People become adrift.

The elders grow silent.

The ceremonies lose meaning.

The community forgets its rhythm.

And in the silence, the people search for themselves.

But how do you find identity when the map has been torn?

How do you find belonging when the story that once told gifted this to us, and now that story has faded?

This isn't just cultural loss, it's a spiritual orphaning.

And in its wake, we see a rise in disorientation, in disconnection, in despair. A collective ache for something we cannot quite name but feel deeply in our bones.

The narrative that once bound us together—threading generations through time—is now fragmented. What remains is longing.

Longing for the ancestors.

Longing for structure.

Longing for meaning.

Longing for a way back.

In this shifting landscape, the once-sturdy pillars of traditional social structures—family hierarchies, communal roles, and intergenerational support—begin to weaken. What follows is a slow erosion of the foundations that once upheld social cohesion. Relationships become fractured. Support networks wither. The tightly woven community begins to unravel, struggling to hold together the stability and interconnectedness that once defined it.

Without the guiding hand of customary laws and time-honoured norms, conflicts become more frequent and more volatile. In the absence of established, trusted mechanisms for resolving disputes, tension festers. The delicate balance that once kept disharmony in check is broken, and in its place rises chaos.

Imagine, if you will, a vast ancestral library—its shelves once teeming with the wisdom of generations. A living archive of knowledge, passed gently from elder to child, story to soul. But as time passes, the doors of this great library are closed. Its halls fall silent. The voices that once echoed within grow faint. And with them, vital skills and insights fade into obscurity. This cultural amnesia leaves behind more than silence—it leaves a void, where rich traditions once lived and breathed.

Traditional economic practices, once woven seamlessly into daily life, begin to fray. These weren't just ways to survive, but ways to honour the land, to connect with nature's rhythms. As these practices decline, so too does economic stability. Communities face mounting challenges adapting to unfamiliar systems, while poverty increases and the gap between old and new becomes harder to bridge.

As the structure collapses, people begin to leave. Individuals, families, and even entire communities seek opportunity and solace elsewhere, resulting in waves of migration and further fragmentation. The diaspora becomes a scattered mosaic—pieces of culture carried into distant places, each struggling to preserve identity in lands far from home.

In the vacuum left by fading traditions, new norms and values begin to rise, often shaped by external forces. While this can spark creativity and adaptation, it also gives rise to tension. The old and the new clash. What emerges is a volatile, ever-shifting terrain where the search for cultural equilibrium becomes a test of resilience and transformation.

This upheaval takes its toll, not only on the structure of society, but on the spirit of its people. The stress of navigating such instability weaves itself into the psyche, manifesting as anxiety, depression, confusion, and grief. As traditional support systems vanish, individuals are left to grapple alone with uncertainty and loss.

Yet, from the ashes of disintegration, a quiet ember may begin to glow. Some communities set forth on a journey to reclaim what has been lost—to rediscover rituals, breathe life back into stories, and adapt ancient practices for a new age. In this collective remembering, there's hope. A spark of pride. A will to survive and transform. The act of cultural revival becomes both resistance and rebirth—a beacon lighting the way through the darkness of cultural decay.

As this grand tapestry unravels, individuals and communities arrive at a powerful crossroads. The breakdown of old structures—while painful—also opens space. Space to reimagine. Space to redefine what it means to belong.

But when this void of purpose, connection, and identity isn't filled with care and wisdom, something else steps in.

Enter gang culture.

In the absence of traditional community structure, gang culture rises to fill the gaps with clarity, order, and belonging. It offers what has been lost: a hierarchy, a code, a place to stand, and people to stand with.

Gangs operate with a clear structure, much like the traditional social systems they replace. At the top are high-ranking leaders or "bosses," making strategic decisions and commanding unwavering loyalty. Beneath them are "underbosses" or senior members who oversee operations and direct lower-ranking individuals. Day-to-day responsibilities fall to these rank-and-file members, while new recruits—known as "wannabes"—spend their early days proving their worth and loyalty.

Rituals and codes take the place of lost ceremonies. Dress codes, tattoos, symbolic gestures—these are the new cultural markers. Initiations and loyalty tests become rites of passage. These aren't just empty acts—they're identity. They're belonging.

Territory replaces ancestral land. Boundaries are drawn not by mountains or rivers, but by graffiti and symbols on walls. Gang presence is marked, defended, and enforced. Control over an area is critical, not just for protection, but for economic influence.

That economy is built on survival. Gangs turn to the trade routes available to them: drug trafficking, illegal gambling, extortion, and robbery. These become not only revenue streams but the basis of power, fuelling operations and commanding influence within and beyond their communities.

And so, in the rubble of dismantled traditions, a new cultural structure forms—born not of ancestry but of absence.

Membership in a gang often begins with an initiation ritual. These rites can range from relatively minor tasks to acts of severe violence. Their purpose is clear: to test loyalty, prove commitment, and bind the individual to the group, not only through action but through allegiance. These rituals reinforce internal values and strengthen cohesion.

Loyalty is the currency of gang culture. Members are expected to obey the hierarchy and adhere strictly to the gang's rules. Discipline is maintained through a mix of incentives and consequences—rewards for obedience, punishment for dissent. Those who stray risk being beaten, banished, or worse.

Yet within this system of control, something very human emerges. Gangs foster powerful social bonds. Members often view one another as family, bound not by blood, but by experience. These relationships are forged in hardship, sustained through shared danger, and built upon the mutual understanding that, in the outside world, belonging is hard to come by.

For those who feel marginalised, rejected, or forgotten, the gang becomes a home. A place to stand. A source of identity. A shield against chaos.

Inter-gang rivalries are common, fuelled by battles for territory, power, and influence. These conflicts are rarely fleeting. They escalate. They retaliate. They spiral into cycles of violence that ripple through communities long after the initial spark has died.

For many, gang life provides a framework—one that offers meaning, structure, and power where none existed before. In the absence of a strong cultural identity or family support, the gang becomes the alternative. It gives voice to the silenced. It gives purpose to the disconnected.

The relationship between gangs and the wider community is complex. In some areas, gangs offer protection, financial support, or social structure where institutions have failed. In others, they're seen as threats—perpetuating crime, fear, and disorder. Community responses range from passive tolerance to outspoken resistance.

At its core, gang culture is built upon a layered system of hierarchy, loyalty, economic survival, and emotional connection. These elements not only influence internal dynamics but also shape how gangs interact with society.

We often ask: *Why are our young so drawn to gang culture?*

My answer is simple: it fills the void left by the collapse of their own cultural identity and structure.

Where once there were elders, now there are bosses.

Where once there were rites of passage, now there are initiations.

Where once there was communal protection, now there is territorial defence.

Where once there was belonging, now there is *belonging with conditions*.

When the village no longer holds the child, the streets will.

In the grand theatre of the animal kingdom, social structures are as diverse as the species themselves—each uniquely shaped by the forces of survival and reproduction. **Their hierarchies aren't arbitrary, but designed to preserve order, cooperation, and continuity within their natural worlds.**

Consider the metropolis of bees. Life within these colonies is a masterclass in specialisation. The queen reigns supreme—her sole purpose, reproduction. Around her buzz the workers, each with a task: some forage, others care for the young, some guard the nest. Male drones serve a reproductive function and little else. Communication isn't verbal but chemical. Pheromones carry messages. Dances direct movement. Every action is synchronised, every rhythm precise.

In the skies, bird societies present another kind of structure. Monogamous pairs—lifelong or seasonal—form teams to nurture, feed and defend their chicks together. In species where territory matters, colourful displays and birdsong mark the borders, warning off rivals.

Then there are birds like pigeons and chickens, which establish strict pecking orders. Dominance dictates access to food, mates, and nesting space. Disputes are settled through gestures and show.

These structures aren't just instinct—they're the architecture of survival. They bring predictability to the unpredictable. They establish order within chaos. And in many ways, they mirror us. Or rather, *we once mirrored them*. Before our structures fractured. Before our cultural scaffolding collapsed.

Imagine the dynamic lives of wolves and lions, where pack life is a finely tuned ballet of roles and responsibilities. At the helm is the alpha pair, steering the pack's destiny, while others contribute to hunting, defending territory, and nurturing the young.

In the world of elephants, matriarchal herds are led by the wisdom of the eldest female. Her guidance ensures the group's survival, drawing on shared care, cooperative parenting, and unwavering support.

Baboons, by contrast, offer a glimpse into a more male-dominated society, where alliances, dominance displays, and social negotiation dictate hierarchy and influence.

Across the primate world, social systems range from the rigid dominance hierarchies of baboons to the egalitarian societies of bonobos. In these communities, age, strength, and social intelligence shape one's standing. Grooming rituals foster tight bonds. Kinship weaves together generations. Cooperation and caregiving are embedded in the very fabric of social life.

Beneath the waves, fish and marine mammals form their own sophisticated networks. Sardines and tuna school together for protection and foraging success. Dolphins and whales live in pods marked by cooperation, shared parenting, and intricate social play. Orcas, or killer whales, live in tightly bonded matriarchal pods, where generations learn and hunt together in stunning synchrony.

Even among insects, there exists a profound social order. Paper wasps, termites, and certain beetles form complex colonies where communication and cooperation are vital. Division of labour ensures the survival of the whole. Each member contributes to the greater good.

And then, there are the solitary ones—tigers and other large cats who roam alone, maintaining vast territories, surfacing only to mate or raise their young.

From the intricate caste systems of social insects to the matriarchal wisdom of elephants, each structure is a masterpiece of adaptation. Every social order, whether communal or solitary, is perfectly tuned to support the survival of the species it serves.

Nature thrives on balance. Harmony. Interdependence.

Which begs the question: **what has gone wrong with us?**

Why are our modern societies plagued by such catastrophic statistics—mental illness, addiction, youth crime, homelessness? Why are people sleeping in parks, alone, frightened, and forgotten?

The quest for power, control, and the almighty dollar has eclipsed our capacity to nurture one another. We celebrate independence over interdependence. We chase prestige over purpose.

We've called this chaos "progress."

But the cost is all around us.

Mental health services are overwhelmed. Addiction is rampant. Families are fragmented. Systems are collapsing under the weight of unmet need.

And yet the solution isn't *rocket science*—a favourite phrase of mine.

The answer lies in honest reflection, in asking how the erosion of cultural structure—our foundations of family, connection, and belonging—has led us here.

This isn't a condemnation of individuals who have contributed great things to the world. It's a reckoning with the slow decay of the very scaffolding that holds societies together.

Because **society isn't thriving**.

Humanity isn't surviving well.

From my Western perspective, I see this clearly: **we're the problem**.

We've tried to recreate health, hierarchy, and wholeness through external constructs—bureaucracies, qualifications, systems—believing these would offer the wisdom we discarded.

But there are two vital shifts we must now embrace.

The first is the **value of family**.

The second is the **value of ancient wisdom**.

During my university years, I came face-to-face with a stark reality: man has elevated himself to a god-like status. Letters after one's name confer a kind of untouchable prestige, a belief that knowledge alone equates to truth. But wisdom without humility is a dangerous thing.

Yes, we need educated minds, but not every wise soul walks out of a university. Some are born of the land, of experience, of pain and community and survival. These people hold influence, too, if we're willing to listen.

What we need now is the **rebuilding of community**.

We must re-establish **shared norms**, hold space for **hierarchies of care**, and restore the sacred value of our elders, women, and children.

We must raise children in environments where clear boundaries and realistic expectations are woven into daily life, not dictated from above but modelled through example.

And we must ask—honestly—**how does throwing millions at a problem actually solve it?**

There are extraordinary people doing extraordinary things— programmes rooted in humanity, offering real solutions to human struggles. But they're small in scale, underfunded, and often overlooked in favour of models that tick boxes but change nothing.

Somewhere along the way, communities adopted a new motto: **"Not my problem."**

People stepped back. Stopped looking. Stopped caring.

But if we refuse to acknowledge our role—if we continue to disengage—we become part of the very systems we criticise.

The evolution of modern man is leading us down a dangerous path: one where ownership is abandoned, engagement dismissed, and responsibility eroded.

It's a path of quiet self-destruction.

Chapter Four

ROLE MODELLING AND INFLUENCERS

"Children learn what they live. So what are we really teaching them?"

The essence of a person emerges as a symphony of complex, intertwining threads, each contributing to the rich, intricate fabric of what it means to be alive. Picture a grand mosaic, where each tile represents a fundamental aspect of human nature coming together to create a vivid, ever-evolving masterpiece.

At the heart of this mosaic lies **self-awareness**—the lens through which we peer into the depths of our own souls. It's a mirror reflecting not just our outward image but the inner landscapes of our thoughts, emotions, and being. This profound introspection bestows upon us a sense of individuality and identity, guiding our journey through the labyrinth of personal growth.

Interwoven with this awareness is our **emotional depth**, coursing through our veins. Our lives are painted with a palette of feelings—vivid strokes of joy and love, sombre shades of sadness and anger. These emotions drive our choices, shape our relationships, fuel our creativity, and colour our sense of fulfilment.

Social connection forms the intricate web that binds us together. As inherently social beings, we're drawn to the warmth of companionship and the strength of community. This need for connection influences the structures of our societies, the norms we uphold, and the way we relate to one another, woven into a tapestry of empathy and collaboration essential to our emotional and psychological health.

Fuelling this connection is our boundless **curiosity and hunger for learning**. Our insatiable quest to explore, understand, and innovate propels us towards new horizons. It's a ceaseless drive that sparks intellectual breakthroughs, artistic wonders, and personal growth, pushing us to expand the boundaries of knowledge and experience.

Beneath this quest lies the guiding compass of **morality and ethics**. Shaped by cultural, religious, and personal values, this moral framework steers our behaviour and interactions. It reflects our deep-seated concerns for justice, fairness, and the well-being of others, providing the moral scaffolding upon which we build our lives.

And yet, it's our **resilience and adaptability** that truly showcase the essence of our spirit. Through trials and tribulations, we demonstrate an extraordinary capacity to rebound and flourish. This resilience enables us to weather the storms of adversity and navigate life's shifting currents with grace and determination.

At the core of our being is a relentless pursuit of **purpose and meaning**. Whether through personal achievements, relationships, spiritual quests, or societal contributions, this search for significance drives us forward, offering direction and motivation as we carve out our place in the world.

Creativity and expression burst forth as a testament to our inner world. Through art, music, literature, and innovation, we channel our thoughts and emotions into forms that reflect our deepest selves. These creative endeavours aren't simply artistic expressions, but windows into the soul, revealing the essence of our lived experience.

And anchoring it all are our primal **biological instincts**—the drives for sustenance, safety, and survival. These instincts intertwine with our cognitive and emotional lives, balancing our most basic needs with our highest aspirations.

In truth, the core of humanity is a multifaceted interplay of self-awareness, emotional richness, social connectivity, intellectual curiosity, moral values, resilience, purpose, creativity, and biological instinct. This intricate blend shapes our experiences, behaviours, and relationships—painting a grand portrait of what it means to be human. An ever-evolving masterpiece, rich with depth and complexity.

Or does it?

From the moment I set foot on Australian soil in 2014, I was met with a disillusionment as immediate as it was profound. My expectations—once lofty—soon crumbled under the weight of harsh reality. The stories of abuse, senseless violence, judgment, blame, and bullying that flood the media are a cruel reminder of this stark contrast.

Across this vast land, a chorus of outrage rings out. People rally against the scourge of bullying. Yet amid the righteous indignation, a tragic story unfolds—a bright and talented young woman, tormented by her peers, succumbs to despair. Her death sparks a cry from heartbroken parents—a plea for justice, a demand to shield the vulnerable from cruelty.

But this outcry, as impassioned as it is, feels like a single drop in an ever-expanding ocean of despair.

What we ignore, we tacitly accept.

This motto echoes loudly as we watch the behaviours of our society from the sidelines, rarely holding up a mirror to our own actions. There's a pervasive tendency to point fingers at schools, systems, and others while conveniently overlooking our own responsibility in shaping the world around us.

On my arrival in Australia, I was taken aback by the media's double standards. A story of bullying is met with stern-faced journalists, hurling words like *"disgusting"* and *"inexcusable."* Yet, in the very next segment, a reporter might be seen hounding an individual with a microphone, demanding, *"What do you have to say about this?"* before that person has even been proven guilty.

Such tactics, cloaked in the guise of journalism, are a form of bullying in themselves. It's absurd to chase someone down with accusations and a camera, as if this is somehow justified in the name of public interest.

The media's relentless pursuit of sensationalism often seems devoid of common sense or accountability. **How can we condemn bullying with one breath, then enact it with the next?** This isn't merely about being *"innocent until proven guilty,"* it's about respect for humanity and recognising where the line should be drawn.

At what point do we regard humanity as inherently worthy of respect? In my book, *all* humanity is worthy of respect, and bad behaviour, while it must be addressed, should be done in a way that nurtures a desire to grow beyond the point we're at.

Our justice system is designed to discern guilt and deliver consequences. Yet media outlets often bypass this principle entirely. We must ask: *Where does public interest end, and basic decency begin?* Many who face media scrutiny are already navigating mental health issues, and public shaming *before* a verdict is reached, which only exacerbates their suffering.

The wider community must model the values we wish to see.

Yet, look no further than parliament. Inside those chambers, the example is appalling—a cacophony of raised voices, jeers, eyerolls, and personal attacks. Politicians, who should embody respect and decorum, instead model pettiness and playground antics. Then they stand before the cameras and present themselves as paragons of virtue.

It's a jarring contrast and far removed from the ideals of respectful discourse.

I reflect on my own upbringing in rural New Zealand. Politics back then—while far from perfect—was something people engaged with. Policy debates were real. Politicians stood for something more than a slogan.

Today, the political landscape resembles a popularity contest. Personality dominates. Policies are mere accessories. Votes are chased not through leadership, but through tactics. And with this shift, the potential for sustainable, meaningful change is steadily undermined.

I've always believed in role modelling. If we want our society to evolve, we must embody the attitudes and behaviours we wish to see in others.

How can we expect respect to flourish when our leaders' model nothing but contempt?

We don't need perfection—we need standards.

Higher expectations.

More conscious conduct.

Because what we're currently modelling as a society is anything but healthy.

Today's world is marked by a glaring absence of respect, a knee-jerk tendency to blame and judge, and a lack of personal accountability. When things go wrong, we single out individuals, rather than interrogating the systems that allow dysfunction to thrive.

At the core of many communities is the belief that punishment is the answer. And yet, despite all this punishment, we see very little in the way of healthy, supportive relationships being built with those who offend or struggle.

Yes, there are those doing this work—quietly, powerfully.

But there are also many who simply tick the boxes.

Do what's easy.

Follow the process.

Avoid the hard stuff.

For me, when I work alongside people who are struggling, I remember a little mantra: **"There but for the grace of God go I."**

When I repeat this to others, I often receive a blank stare.

"That's not me."

"That would never be me."

But the truth is, we're all closer to the edge than we like to believe.

> **The breakdown in community structure has left many without positive role models or influencers.**

In shadowed corners of countless households, silent influences take root, shaping young minds in ways that often go unnoticed.

The impact of **unhealthy male role modelling** seeps into the lives of boys and girls alike, leaving a trail that stretches far beyond childhood.

Picture a young boy—wide-eyed and eager—looking up to his father or the men around him. He absorbs their actions and words, both good and bad, like a sponge.

If what he sees is aggression, emotional detachment, or indifference, he learns that these are the ways a man behaves.

When he's upset, he's told to, *"Man up,"* or that, *"Boys don't cry."*

He begins to believe that vulnerability is weakness, that strength lies in silence or violence.

As he grows, these lessons become ingrained.

At school, he might become the bully or the silent boy who never speaks.

At work, he may struggle to connect, mistaking assertiveness for aggression.

In relationships, he may fear expressing emotion, believing it will lead to ridicule or rejection.

Unhealthy male role models teach boys that toughness means suppression.

That kindness is weakness.

That empathy is unmanly.

But the damage doesn't stop with boys.

Young girls absorb these behaviours, too. They learn to expect emotional unavailability. They witness aggression and come to see it as normal. Many girls today are alongside, the bullying, the verbal and physical violence, against other girls, and dismiss these things with a sense of entitlement.

In relationships, they may seek out emotionally distant partners, mirroring the dynamics they watched unfold in childhood.

The impact of unhealthy male and female role modelling is both **subtle and far-reaching**.

It quietly weaves itself into how women and men experience the world—how they assess their worth, how they interpret power, and how they navigate love, trust, and safety.

It shapes the lens through which they view others, relationships, and themselves.

Imagine a young girl growing up in an environment where the men around her model masculinity as dominance, control, or emotional unavailability. She learns, early and often, that men are to be feared or appeased, not understood or trusted.

Her first lessons in what to expect from men are coloured by aggression or indifference. These early imprints often become the blueprint for her future interactions.

As she grows, these formative experiences may manifest in countless ways.

In her personal relationships she might find herself drawn to men who mirror the behaviours she witnessed in childhood—controlling, dismissive, emotionally distant. Consciously or not, she may come to believe that this is what love looks like. That a man's anger is passion. That his silence is a challenge she must meet with more of her own emotional labour.

In the workplace or social settings the echoes of unhealthy male role modelling might lead her to downplay her achievements, to defer to male colleagues, or to remain silent in the face of disrespect. The silent teachings of her upbringing—that men hold the power, that their actions are not to be questioned—can settle over her like an invisible weight, muting her confidence and limiting her voice.

For young men, who grow up with mothers who struggle, they too can gain a distorted view of women. In traditional times – women had close connection with other women, they supported each other in the ups and downs of life, and men were supported by older healthy men in the tribe. Men nor women were expected to understand and support men's business or women's business – today men and women often struggle to meet each other's needs.

But this impact isn't confined to the individual. It ripples outward, shaping societal norms, entrenching gender roles, and reinforcing systems where women must adapt, endure, and navigate a world that often undervalues their contributions.

When unhealthy male or female role models dominate, they do more than harm relationships—they help build a culture that normalises harm. A culture that rewards detachment in men and resilience in women. A culture that reinforces the idea that women must bend themselves around the behaviours of men, or visa-versa, instead of both learning to relate from a place of mutual understanding.

And yet, within this narrative of harm, there's the potential for profound change.

Women, so often through their own quiet resistance and fierce resilience, are leading that change. By demanding respect. By modelling boundaries. By embracing emotional intelligence and rejecting outdated notions of what it means to be a man or a woman, they're rewriting the rules. Unfortunately, this runs a risk of all men being stigmatised and labelled, which is not true. There are many amazing, grounded caring men, who have these qualities, and are masculine in their sense of self and their values.

Unhealthy male role modelling affects women deeply—sometimes visibly, sometimes invisibly. But naming this truth is the first step towards transformation. By recognising how these models have shaped us all, we begin the process of dismantling them. And in that dismantling, we create space for something new. Something more whole.

A future where men and women alike are free to be human. To be seen. To be safe in their expression. To be truly themselves.

The ripple effects of unhealthy male role modelling can stretch through generations, weaving cycles of misunderstanding, resentment, and pain. But there's always a glimmer of hope.

Change begins the moment we choose to see. To question. To rewrite the script.

By fostering healthier male role models—men who show that strength lies in vulnerability, that leadership comes with empathy, and that masculinity isn't threatened by kindness—we create a new template.

When men model patience, emotional literacy, and compassion, they teach the next generation that true strength lies not in domination, but in connection.

In this new narrative, the shadow begins to fade. And in its place rises a brighter, more inclusive story—one where all people, regardless of gender, learn to thrive, love, and lead with authenticity.

Chapter Five

THE EROSION OF EMPOWERMENT

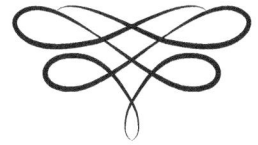

*"When systems silence the soul,
the spark of hope begins to fade."*

"I just don't know what to do."

The familiar refrain echoes—a desperate confession from countless voices, each one more exhausted than the last. *"I've tried everything to change this, but nothing changes."*

This isn't just the voice of one individual. It's the cry of a society that has lost its way—a society tangled in a system that stands tall like an ivory tower, its foundations quietly crumbling beneath the weight of decades of cultural decay.

The erosion of empowerment—of self-reliance—hasn't come in a single catastrophic moment. It has been gradual, relentless. Like a tide, it has swept away the shore grain by grain.

And who stands to blame for this decay?

The system would have you believe it holds the answers. That salvation lies within its bureaucracy. That the solutions are found in its frameworks, forms, and funding models.

But real people—those who once stood proud, supporting themselves, their families, and their communities—have slowly swallowed a different story. They've been told, again and again, that it's the government's responsibility to solve their problems. That it's the government's burden to carry society's well-being.

But under the crushing weight of these expectations, the system is buckling.

The very institutions designed to support are straining. The issues draining life from our communities—violence, addiction, mental health, homelessness— are not only defeating individuals, they're defeating the government itself, though few will ever admit it.

The battle for positive outcomes? It was lost before it even began.

And still, the system persists—throwing money at broken scaffolds, duplicating failed strategies, hoping that, *maybe this time*, something will shift.

They hold press conferences.

Smile.

Pat themselves on the back.

"Look at us. Aren't we doing well?"

In September 2024, the government announced another bold initiative—a massive financial pledge to halve the rates of family violence by 2031.

A $4.4 billion national plan to end violence against women and children (Commonwealth of Australia, 2022). $47 million to frontline services for women and children. Millions more for recovery, early intervention, workforce development, and specialist training. (https://www.dss.gov.au/national-plan)

But as the numbers stack up, one thing becomes clear: these are figures on a page. Dollars assigned, not outcomes achieved.

And while investment in education and awareness is important, we've seen it before. Just as we have with mental health and domestic violence, *awareness* alone doesn't solve the deeper, more insidious issues at play.

People are more aware of their mental health than ever before. More are seeking help. But underneath this awareness lies a hollow belief—ingrained over years—that *recovery*, true recovery, is a far-off dream. That once a person is broken, they stay broken.

The tools we've been handed to tackle these issues?

They're the same rusty instruments we've used for decades.

A prescription for medication.

A few sessions of cognitive behavioural therapy.

Psychoeducation delivered by a registered psychologist with the backing of "evidence-based practice."

I've been told more times than I can count that this research is sacred, unchallengeable. The gospel by which we must all operate.

And yet…I've seen it fail. Repeatedly.

I remember standing toe-to-toe with a head psychiatrist, who insisted—without hesitation—that he knew everything there was to know about a particular client's diagnosis.

"You know nothing," he told me, with a wave of his hand and a look of disdain.

Why?

Because I had dared to challenge his methods. To question the script. To ask if perhaps the human being in front of us deserved to be seen, not just diagnosed.

"We are the experts," he said, perched on his pedestal of credentials.

But what he couldn't see—what he wouldn't see—was the person standing before him. Not a case file. Not a diagnosis. Not a label. But a life. A soul.

For all their learning, for all their textbooks and titles, they had become blind.
Lost in the brilliance of their own qualifications. And in doing so, the truth—the *humanity*—slipped through their fingers.

Broken Families, Broken Systems, Broken Promises
The Erosion of Empowerment

I often find myself replaying one particular meeting that's etched into my mind like a scene I cannot unsee.

It was a case review. The psychiatrist was present. So was I, supporting both the young man at the centre of the discussion and his mother, who had endured so much at the hands of the mental health system.

This young man—brilliant, creative, misunderstood. His mother—exhausted, devoted, desperate for someone to truly listen.

Thanks to the magic of telehealth, I joined the review remotely, ready to help guide them through the clinical maze. My role was to bridge the gap—translate the jargon, hold space, and ensure the plan was actually informed by truth.

But it didn't take long for things to go wrong.

The psychiatrist launched in, relentlessly pressing the importance of the young man's medication.

Now, I'd worked with this young man for close to 18 months. When we first met, he had no awareness of his condition. He was on a community treatment order (CTO) required by law to receive his injection every fortnight.

He had made progress—real progress. But he had never once viewed his experiences through the lens of mental illness. The voice he heard? To him, it wasn't a symptom. It was real. It had meaning. It made sense in the world he knew.

And in that moment, faced with a man in a white coat dictating treatment, he shrank back—not just in body, but in spirit.

Because what was unfolding wasn't care. It was control.

As the psychiatrist continued to press his agenda, the familiar power struggle surfaced. He demanded the young man acknowledge the voice he heard—to admit it was a symptom, proof of his illness and evidence that medication was essential.

But the client held firm. He had always been consistent in his belief. The voice wasn't a product of illness; it had meaning. It served a purpose. It came from something beyond himself—a force, a presence, something real to him.

Rather than listening, the psychiatrist grew agitated. His patience wore thin until, with a patronising tone that made my skin crawl, he said: **"I hope one day you'll mature and see the need for medication."**

In that moment, the entire atmosphere shifted. The young man's body tensed. You could see it—his jaw clenched, his shoulders tightened. Anger simmered just below the surface, ready to boil over. I couldn't stay silent.

"You don't have to sit here and take this abuse," I told them, voice firm. *"Let's go."*

But it wasn't that simple. The room might not have had bars, but it was still a prison—gated, controlled. They couldn't simply walk out. They needed permission.

By the time they were finally allowed to leave, the damage had been done. The young man was a storm—fuming, humiliated, powerless. His mother was distraught. Heartbroken.

She'd seen it all before—cold, clinical cruelty dressed up as care. That day unravelled everything we had worked towards over the past 18 months.

I had walked with him through the darkest days—through substance dependence, self-doubt, and the relentless voice that never gave him peace. I had never dismissed his reality. Never told him he was wrong, broken, or deluded.

We worked *with* his experience. We built a plan around *his* goals, not mine, not the system's. And in that time, he achieved more than many thought possible.

10 months clean.

No substances.

A clear vision for the future.

He wanted off the medication—not recklessly, but responsibly. He wanted out of the mental health system. He wanted freedom from the community treatment order that bound him to fortnightly injections.

You might assume his mother and I were reckless, that we encouraged him to stop medication, but that couldn't be further from the truth. We all understood that the medication had played an important role. The issue wasn't its existence—it was the dosage. The overwhelming side effects. The way it dulled his spark.

We supported the idea of reduction, not elimination. We respected the importance of treatment, but we also respected his right to have a say. Yet every report from mental health services told a different story.

In their version, we were undermining his treatment.

Blocking his progress.

Standing in the way.

But the truth is, we had created a plan together—one he believed in. It allowed him to remain clean and compliant with medication while moving towards autonomy.

He was hopeful. Empowered.

His next tribunal hearing for the CTO was approaching, and he planned to request a trial without it, promising to continue medication, but on his own terms. To him, that wasn't about rejecting treatment. It was about reclaiming control. It was about dignity.

But that single meeting—with that single psychiatrist—shattered everything.

What could have been a moment of shared progress became a moment of emotional violence. A power play. A dismissal.

All because someone refused to see the person standing in front of them.

The systems talk a big game.

They speak of *"collaboration"* like it's a warm blanket wrapped around every client.

They preach *"client-centred care"* as though saying the words is enough.

They tout statistics. Funding. The numbers coming through the doors.

But they don't talk about the ones who never return.

The ones who fall through the cracks.

The ones who lose faith.

Or worse—the ones trapped in the revolving door, spinning in and out, over and over, caught in a loop with no real way out.

> **My question is simple, but it cuts deep:**
> ***"In what universe is it acceptable to place the blame solely on the client, while never reflecting on the forces that shape their spiral of unwellness?"***

You'd think the answer would be obvious: *none*.

But here we are. Living in a world where clinicians are exalted as infallible experts, while clients—and their families—are painted as problematic, non-compliant, or uncooperative.

In my work—whether in mental health, addiction, domestic violence, or behaviour change—I see it far too often.

A staggering lack of insight into what real change takes.

A refusal to value the lived experience.

A complete disregard for the human being struggling across the table.

These systems don't just fail individuals.

They fail families.

They fail communities.

And I've fought this battle, not just as a professional, but as a *person*. As someone who cares.

Since colonisation, since the wars, since the rise of globalisation, we've watched community structures crumble.

We've watched families disintegrate—torn apart by well-meaning laws that protect individual rights, but often at the cost of connection, care, and commonsense.

We've lost the old ways. The collective ways. The understanding that *when one suffers, we all do.*

The focus on individual autonomy, however noble, has come at a cost. Family members are pushed to the sidelines. Sometimes ostracised. Treated as barriers rather than bridges.

Broken Families, Broken Systems, Broken Promises
The Erosion of Empowerment

I remember one case—a family member, thousands of miles away, trying desperately to get help for an adult child suffering from psychosis. They weren't asking for control. They were asking to be heard. To be involved. To support.

But the system shut them out.

It was a morning soaked in fear. The family knew something was terribly wrong. Their adult child was homeless, battling addiction, and had severed ties with them, accusing them of not caring. But now, she had sent a letter—a letter filled with dark intent, explaining her decision to end it all.

Panic surged. The family called for help. Five separate calls to emergency services, each one a painful repetition of the same desperate details. Eventually, the message reached the correct police department—the one covering the area where the at-risk woman had last been seen. But even then, they were met with a cold, bureaucratic wall.

"What's the address?" they asked.

"She's homeless," the family replied.

"Sorry, we can't help."

Imagine hearing those words—knowing someone you love is out there, lost in despair—and the very system meant to protect her simply shrugs its shoulders.

"Don't tell me you can't help," the family member demanded. *"She's known to you. She's on your radar."*

Only after that outcry did the system stir. 10 minutes later, a call came through. The police had found her.

The family could breathe—*but only for a moment.*

Because this story, like so many others, didn't end there.

She was taken to the hospital. But once inside, the familiar routine played out. The doctors demanded proof of risk. The family handed over the letter, a heartbreaking manifesto of hopelessness.

And still, despite her words written in black and white, she was allowed to self-discharge. Their judgement? She was no longer a risk. Not a threat to herself or anyone else.

Imagine, if you will, someone suffering a heart attack. Would the system respond so casually? So callously? Would they allow that person to walk out of the emergency department simply because the pain had temporarily eased?

But mental health and addiction? That's a different beast. The blame is easier to lay at the feet of the individual or their family. It's easier to say, *"They don't want to change,"* than it is to ask why the system keeps failing them.

I've seen it time and again. Families, broken and exhausted, bringing their loved ones to the hospital, waiting hours only to be turned away. These families aren't supported. They're not empowered. They're worn down, told to carry the unbearable weight of responsibility for someone else's life, while professionals—the very people meant to help—turn their backs.

Broken Families, Broken Systems, Broken Promises
The Erosion of Empowerment

And then comes the chorus of blame:

"They're self-sabotaging."

"They don't really want help."

"The family is enabling them."

These are the judgments that echo through the corridors of hospitals and clinics every single day.

It's not just mental health and addiction. Look at domestic and family violence.

Women—desperate for safety—sometimes return to the very relationships that broke them. And instead of compassion, they're met with disdain: *"Why doesn't she just leave?"* As if the solution were simple.

Rebuilding a life after violence is a monumental task. One that falls squarely on the woman's shoulders. And the perpetrator? He might be fined. He might serve some time. But his life? It continues. For him, there's always another woman. Another unsuspecting victim.

I've lost count of how many times I've seen police return violent men to the family home.

I've stood beside terrified mothers watching officers escort their son, fully grown and well-built, back into the house.

"He's promised to behave," they say.

It's an impossible situation.

The cells are full.

Mental health wants nothing to do with it.

And the mother? She's left with guilt, fear, and no support.

Because at the end of the day, this is her son. And who else is going to care for him?

We talk about systems.

We talk about professionals.

We talk about processes.

But until we start talking about *people*, nothing will change.

Families need support.

Communities need to feel empowered.

> **And the arrogance, judgment, and ignorance that plagues our institutions need to be stripped away.**
>
> **Until that happens, we're just spinning in circles, passing the blame like a baton in a race no one ever wins.**

PART THREE

THE URGENCY OF CHANGE

"The system is broken. The damage is real. The truth is undeniable—addiction, criminal justice, domestic and family violence, youth crime, and mental health services aren't failing by accident. They're failing by design."

Billions are poured into these systems year after year with little to show for it. We've walked through the evidence together: the failures of well-funded programmes, the hollow promises of policies, and the false hope of strategies that barely scratch the surface of these so-called wicked problems. And the cost? It's not just numbers on a balance sheet—it's the devastation of families, communities, and entire generations.

Despite this relentless funding the outcomes remain the same. At best, we see temporary relief. At worst, nothing changes at all. The cycles of despair continue to turn, the chaos persists, and still, we bear witness to a system that simply doesn't work.

I've shared the raw truth; the statistics, the stories, the lived experiences of those trapped in the revolving door of systemic failure. The question is no longer, "Does the system work?" because we know it doesn't. The real question is: What are we going to do about it?

Change is no longer an option—it's an obligation. There's no room for small cosmetic adjustments. What we need now is a radical shift, a reimagining, one that flips the power structure on its head. But here lies the greatest barrier: those holding the power have no real incentive to change. Why would they? Their positions are secure, their pay guaranteed, and their systems self-protecting.

In all my years I've met only a handful of brave, visionary leaders within the system—people who recognise that the current model is broken beyond repair. They, too, are frustrated. But their rare, often isolated voices are drowned out by the machinery of status quo thinking.

When a scandal hits the headlines the response is predictable: public outrage, a formal enquiry, a string of well-rehearsed statements, and the familiar appointment of those who helped build the system in the first place. Then, we wait, only to receive reports that confirm what families already knew, and watch as recommendations are shelved, underfunded, or quietly ignored.

Here's the hard truth:

You can't build a better future with the same minds that created the past. And you certainly can't fix the system by asking those who have never lived its failures to redesign it.

In a structure where leaders are rewarded for stability—not innovation—there's no appetite to think outside the box. And so, the wheel keeps turning, and families keep falling through the cracks.

But there's hope. It just doesn't start where you might expect.

The path forward isn't top-down. It's bottom-up. Real change must rise through the very people who have been left behind—individuals, families, and communities who know, through painful lived experience, what isn't working. They're not the problem. They're the answer.

We must stop waiting for permission.

We must stop hoping the system will fix itself.

Instead, we begin with what we already have: people. Stories. Strength. Community.

The solution isn't sweeping reform from above—it's empowerment from below. Real, lasting transformation starts with one person, one family, one community at a time. When we equip people to take ownership, speak a new language of change, and stand strong in the face of despair, we create ripple effects that disrupt the current, shift the tide, and bring about true impact.

We can no longer afford to keep investing in systems that maintain dysfunction. Now is the time to invest in people. In possibility. In a future that honours the pain and turns it into power.

What follows isn't just a vision—it's a map.

In the next five chapters, you'll discover the framework I use to create real, sustainable change—grounded in lived experience, backed by results, and centred on the people who matter most. Each chapter offers a practical, powerful step toward shifting the tide from chaos to clarity, from fear to strength, from helplessness to hope.

If you've ever felt the weight of a broken system pressing down on your clients, your family, or your own spirit…this is where you'll find a new way forward.

This is where the change begins.

Chapter One

ANCIENT FOUNDATION, MODERN COMPASS

*"We cannot walk backwards into the past,
but we can bring this ancient wisdom into today."*

We cannot walk backwards into the past. The world that once was—of sacred fires, ancestral chants, and land as kin—isn't a place we can return to. Colonisation carved deep wounds, not only in the soil, but in the very spirit of how we understand wellness, family, and healing.

But the wisdom? The wisdom never left.

Across oceans and continents, long before the word 'wellbeing' was ever coined, entire civilisations lived by frameworks that honoured the whole person—body, mind, spirit, and community.

These weren't bullet points on a poster. They were ways of life. Passed down in chants and stories, lived out in ceremonies and obligations, these teachings formed the heartbeat of cultures that knew you cannot separate a person from their land, people, or purpose.

The model I carry forward in my work isn't a replica of the past. It's a modern compass, guided by ancient stars. It stands on four cornerstones: physical, psychological, social, and spiritual. These aren't new ideas. They're old truths remembered.

My model brings back the values of old—with the 'collective community' being a foundation of well-being—not the individualism that Western cultures promote and encourage.

Before the Western World: Remembering the Ancestors of the Isles
It's easy to think of Indigenous wisdom as something that belongs only to faraway lands, but we must not forget that those of English, Irish, Scottish and Celtic heritage also walked with a deep sense of connection, long before empires and industrial conquest.

Over 2,000 years ago, the ancient peoples of the British Isles lived close to the land. The Celts, Picts, and Druids of Ireland and Gaul also followed the rhythms of the sun and moon, the wheel of the year marked by solstices, equinoxes, fire festivals and harvest rites.

Their spiritual wellness was anchored in sacred groves, stone circles, wells, rivers and whispering forests. They communed with nature spirits, honoured the elements, and believed in the thinning of the veil between worlds, especially during times like Samhain, when the spirit world and human world could meet.

Their healing systems included plant medicine, ritual bathing, chanting, and offerings to the gods and goddesses of earth, sky, and water. The ban-draoi (female Druids) and ollamhs (wisdom keepers) played the role of healer, poet, historian, and spiritual guide. They didn't separate body from soul. They understood that disease often came from spiritual misalignment or broken ties within the clan.

Social well-being was embedded in tribe and kin. Brehon laws, which governed early Irish life, showed a people deeply concerned with honour, reciprocity, and the protection of community. Decisions were made in council. Elders held wisdom. Oral storytelling passed values through generations, and hospitality was a sacred duty.

We may not wear cloaks of wool or carve standing stones today, but in our blood—our bones—we carry this memory. The loss of these practices wasn't natural. It came with conquest, Christianity's spread, and later colonisation. But the ember still glows.

Reclaiming wellness through this lens isn't about romanticising the past. It's about re-remembering that even in the Western world, there was once balance. There was once reverence. There was once rhythm.

We don't need to borrow well-being from faraway cultures. We can return to the ancient teachings buried in our own lineage—and let them speak again, in ways our modern world so desperately needs.

From the Whare: The Māori Model of Hauora
In Aotearoa, the Māori people have long known that a person's health is like a house. Te Whare Tapa Whā (Durie, 1985) is the model passed down through generations—a whare (house) with four walls:

- ❖ **Taha Tinana:** the physical body, nurtured through food, rest, traditional medicine and movement.
- ❖ **Taha Hinengaro:** the mental and emotional world, woven through self-awareness, storytelling, and cultural identity.
- ❖ **Taha Whānau:** the social wall, reinforced by kinship, shared responsibility, and collective care.
- ❖ **Taha Wairua:** the spiritual self, bound to land, ancestors, and unseen forces that carry us through life.

Māori healing practices like rongoā (plant-based medicine) weren't just physical remedies. A healer, or tohunga, would also use karakia (sacred prayer) to lift the spirit, restore mauri (life force), and call on ancestors to surround the unwell with strength.

In this worldview, disconnection is illness. When one wall weakens, the whole whare leans. When someone is struggling, the answer is rarely individual. The answer is whānau. Although many know and understand this model, and do model services by Māori, for Māori, there's one thing I know: modern day Western culture has yet to shift into what works for Māori—works for Pākehā (non-Polynesian New Zealanders) too.

When exploring Western models, it's clear that they don't work for anyone! We can't go back to traditional marae life, but we can ask: what does it look like to rebuild all four walls in our modern lives?

The Dreaming (Stanner, 1979): **An Aboriginal Way of Seeing**
For the Aboriginal and Torres Strait Islander peoples, wellness isn't just a personal state—it's country, kin, and culture. Their model of health is known today as social and emotional wellbeing (SEWB) (Gee et al., 2014), but it's ancient in origin.

At the heart of it is connection:
- ❖ To body, cared for through bush medicine and balanced living.
- ❖ To mind, strengthened by dadirri (deep listening) (Ungunmerr-Baumann, 2002) and dreaming stories.
- ❖ To family and kin, who share responsibilities and pass down culture.
- ❖ To spirit, held through ceremony and the sacred bond with the land.

The dreaming isn't just a myth; it's a living law. Songlines crisscross the land like spiritual arteries, guiding people with stories encoded in earth and sky. Everything has meaning. Everything has memory.

Healing comes through ceremony—like smoking rituals to cleanse, or the laying of hands by Ngangkari healers who see beyond the body to the soul.

Disconnection from country, story, or your role is illness. Healing is returning. We may not return to a world of corroborees around the campfire, but we can listen. Deeply. We can find our own songline—a path that brings us home to who we truly are.

NB: The concepts of The Dreaming, Dadirri, and Ngangkari healing belong to specific Aboriginal communities and nations. While referenced here with care, they are not universal to all Aboriginal or Torres Strait Islander peoples.

The Sacred Circle: Native American Medicine Wheel
There is no single origin for the Medicine Wheel, as it is a living spiritual framework passed down orally across many First Nations People. However, for those who want to explore more, one of the most widely respected published interpretations for academic or cross-cultural referencing is by *Angeles Arrien (1993)*.

Across the vast lands, the Indigenous peoples of North America shaped their well-being around the Medicine Wheel. This circle of life honours four quadrants:

- **Physical:** sustained through sacred food, herbal medicine, and movement.
- **Mental:** shaped through story, learning, and reflection.
- **Emotional:** nurtured through community, humour, and shared ceremony.
- **Spiritual:** deepened by prayer, vision quests, and reverence for the Creator.

The circle is sacred. It teaches that everything is connected—the four directions, seasons, and stages of life. To be healthy is to be in balance. When imbalance arises, ceremony is the remedy: sweat lodges for purification, pipe rituals for prayer, and songs that carry the spirit back into harmony.

Healing isn't private. It's a community act. When one hurts, all respond. When one rejoices, all give thanks. Storytelling, too, is medicine—through trickster tales, creation stories, and ancestral myths, people learn how to live, grieve, and hope.

In today's world, we may not gather in tipi circles or follow buffalo across the plains, but we can walk in beauty. We can let the Medicine Wheel remind us that healing isn't linear. It's circular. It's relational.

Modern Compass, Ancient Stars
The model I live by in my personal and professional life isn't about going back. We cannot replant what colonisation uprooted, but we can re-root ourselves. In story. In land. In kinship. In meaning.

These cultures teach us that:

- ❖ Physical health is more than fitness.
- ❖ Emotional wellness is held in connection, not control.
- ❖ Healing happens in circles, not isolation.
- ❖ Spiritual strength is found in the whispers of ancestors and the rhythms of the earth.

We carry these teachings forward—not as imitation, but as inspiration. We're building new vessels for old truths.

The Inner Compass Code™ isn't a replica of ancient systems. But it's deeply informed by them. It honours the four winds of wellness, not as separate strategies, but as a map back to wholeness.

Because when we remember what was true then, we remember what can still be true now. And with that remembering, we can chart a new course.

Reframing the System: Applying Ancient Wisdom to Modern-Day Challenges

If ancient wisdom taught us that well-being is found in connection, story, rhythm and restoration, then the systems we've inherited—and the ones we continue to build—must be asked the hard question: what have we forgotten?

In a world that measures time in dollars and healing in diagnoses, we must become fluent again in the language of balance.

Healthcare: Modern healthcare too often treats the symptom, not the story. A person walks into a clinic with chest pain and walks out with pills, but no one asks about the weight of their grief, the burden of their disconnection, or the isolation that pounds louder than any heartbeat.

What if every health service began with dadirri—deep listening? What if a GP had access to a local elder, a storytelling space, and a garden of native medicine plants?

We need healthcare that's community-held, where the land is part of healing, and where cultural connection isn't an afterthought, but a foundation. We can learn from rongoā, sweat lodges, and the very idea that healing is sacred, not scheduled.

Education: Our schools still too often reward silence, compliance, and academic rigidity. Yet, in traditional cultures, children learned through experience, storytelling, and their place within a tribe. They were apprenticed into identity before they were tested on achievement.

Imagine schools that taught through circles, not rows. That opened the day with karakia, welcomed emotion as part of learning, and embedded ancestral stories into science, maths, and literature.

Let us teach our children that wellness is more than marks. It's knowing who you are, where you come from, and how to walk with others.

Justice: Punishment has become the default in modern systems, but traditional justice was often based on restoration. Elders, ceremonies, and community truth-telling held those who harmed accountable—not to shame them, but to call them back into connection.

What would happen if we replaced solitary confinement with circle sentencing? If prisons became places of cultural learning, skill-building, and healing, places where the four winds of the Medicine Wheel could be brought into balance?

Justice systems shouldn't break people further. They should help them remember their place in the story.

Social Services and Family Support: Western models often focus on fixing individuals. But in Indigenous traditions, it's the collective that holds the power to restore.

What if instead of sending in a caseworker to "manage a case," we built community teams—whānau, elders, cultural guides—who could help families remember their own strength?

Let us move from transactional support to transformational relationships. Let us understand that when someone is struggling, it may not be because they're weak, but because the village is missing.

Mental Health: Rather than seeing anxiety and depression as personal flaws, traditional frameworks often viewed emotional pain as a call to realignment with the land, values, and ancestry. The Night Chant of the Navajo, the healing hands of the Ngangkari, the quiet forest walks of Māori practice—they weren't luxuries. They were lifelines.

In a time when mental health is in crisis, we must return to the wisdom that says: healing isn't found only in talk, but in ceremony, connection, and the rhythms of the natural world.

A Future Rooted in the Past
The path ahead isn't paved with nostalgia. It's lit by memory. These ancient frameworks aren't just cultural artefacts—they're blueprints for systems that work. Systems that honour the whole. Systems that remember that to care for one is to care for all.

Our challenge isn't to mimic, but to translate. To take the songline and make it sing in classrooms. To take the circle and make it the boardroom. To take the tohunga and welcome their wisdom into clinics and councils.

Because the truth is: we've always known how to heal, and it was never alone.

So let us bring the old teachings into new places. Let us reframe not just our services, but our thinking. Let us walk forward—together—with the compass of our ancestors and the courage to change what no longer serves.

Because when we remember how we once lived well, we unlock the power to do so again.

Humanity has somehow lost its way and is continuing to destroy the very things that are important. Our place to belong, not only on our land but within our communities and families. Our sense of purpose has been dissolved, and humanity has destroyed its very foundations of wellness and well-being. When it comes to westernised values, we only value our 'head,' and that's one thing that's behind every issue we face today.

Humanity isn't broken. It's simply buried deep within. Let's dig. Let's listen. Let's rise.

> ***Together, let us remember: healing isn't new. It's old. It's sacred. And it still lives within us; we just need to connect and feed it, so humanity can once again move toward wellness.***

Chapter Two

FROM DISEMPOWERMENT TO EMPOWERMENT

"Why connection is the most powerful force for change."

There's a quiet myth running through the heart of every modern care system. It whispers to families—desperate, frightened, and clinging to hope—that the answer lies in someone else. That if they can just get their loved one into the right hands, with the right expert, at the right time, everything will turn around.

We're taught, almost from the moment we ask for help, to seek solutions externally. Doctors, counsellors, caseworkers, crisis teams—we hand our loved ones' lives over, believing the system is designed to catch them. This isn't foolishness. It's what we've been told. It's how we've been conditioned to respond in the face of addiction, mental illness, or crisis: find a professional. Let them fix it.

And so, **families become spectators to the struggle, watching from the shore as the one they love is swept further into chaos.**

They wait for appointments. They research services. They put their faith in clinical pathways. But in reality? Most of those in crisis never make it through the door. Many who do, don't stay, and even among those who engage, the outcomes are often fragile, inconsistent, and unsustainable.

Professionals—good ones—know this. They've read the research, sat with the failure, and felt the heartbreak too. Many know that the single most powerful predictor of change isn't technique or policy—it's relationship. And yet, when change doesn't happen, the mirror is rarely turned inward. Instead, the failure is assigned back to the client and the family. They didn't follow through. They didn't enforce boundaries. They enabled. They got in the way.

But what if the problem isn't the family at all? What if the real problem is that we never truly empowered them in the first place?

> **"We indoctrinate families to believe someone else will fix it—then blame them when no one can."**

What if, instead of sidelining the very people holding the relationship, we saw them as the key?

Most healing doesn't happen in rooms marked "therapy." It happens in kitchens, on couches, or during 3 a.m. text messages. It happens in the middle of anger and heartbreak, in the quiet moments after another broken promise, in the pause before deciding whether to yell or listen. Families are already in the room where the real moments happen. The professionals aren't. I'm not. Your loved one isn't sitting in front of me. In fact, most of the time, they don't even believe they have a problem. But you're there, and that makes you the best person to influence change. Not to fix it, but to shape the space in which change can grow.

This doesn't mean the burden is yours to carry alone. Quite the opposite. **Empowerment isn't about more responsibility.** It's about reclaiming influence, understanding that while you cannot control another person, you can shape the conditions around them. You can build a relational bridge strong enough to hold weight, wide enough to invite return, and steady enough to withstand the storms.

Decades of research confirm this: whether in mental health or addiction settings, the strength of the relationship is the most consistent predictor of positive change. Not the diagnosis. Not the strategy. Not the script. It's the connection between two people—one reaching out, and the other choosing to stay in the room.

Therapists and professionals are trained to build these alliances. We assume they know the importance of empathy, shared goals, and emotional safety. Therapists and other professionals' benefit when they're tracking the health of the relationship, repairing ruptures, and reflecting on their role when things stall. This isn't always done; the easiest marker of success in this relationship is someone's continued engagement. There will always be an ebb and flow when it comes to change; knowing this and responding to it in a beneficial way makes a difference.

Yet here's the paradox. Even as professionals are trained in theory, relationship, and empathy, many remain disconnected from their own Inner Compass. Not by choice, but by design. Systems don't nurture wholeness in the healer. They demand productivity, compliance, and outcomes that can be measured in tick boxes. They reward head-based knowledge while neglecting the heart and gut—the very places where wisdom, intuition, and connection live.

The truth is that most professionals are under immense pressure. They're buried under caseloads, battling burnout, and operating within structures that value throughput over transformation. They know what good practice looks like, but rarely have the time, space, or support to live it out. They're asked to carry the pain of others while being denied the space to process their own.

So, they fall back on the safe, the structured, the manualised. Not because they don't care, but because the system teaches them to lead with their head and leave the rest at the door.

But healing doesn't come from the head alone. It never has.

When a professional is disconnected from their own Inner Compass, their practice becomes transactional, not transformational. They may know the theory of relationships, but they cannot embody it. They may deliver the right words, but the energy behind them is hollow. Clients feel that. Families feel that. And so the revolving door turns again.

If we want real change, we must first reconnect the professionals to themselves. To their values. To the deep, ancient knowing that drew them into this work to begin with. We need practitioners who work not just from knowledge, but from alignment.

Because when we anchor into our Inner Compass™—head, heart, and gut working as one—our presence becomes the intervention. And that kind of presence cannot be outsourced. It must be lived.

Now let's widen the lens.

For every one person caught in addiction, mental illness, or crisis, there are at least nine others who are directly affected. Parents. Siblings. Partners. Children. Friends. Neighbours. Co-workers. The system barely registers them. It views them as collateral, or at best, secondary. But these nine aren't just bystanders—they're potential changemakers. They're the ones holding the stories, the grief, the impact. And they're the ones with the greatest reach into the everyday reality of the person who's struggling.

If we reimagined our systems through this lens—not just serving the one but empowering the nine—everything would change.

Imagine a mental health service where family sessions aren't offered as an afterthought but embedded as standard. Where the first question isn't, "What's wrong with the client?" but "Who are the people around them, and how can we strengthen those relationships?"

Imagine an addiction treatment program that doesn't just focus on sobriety, but on restoring relational ecosystems—equipping mothers, partners, and children with the tools to stay steady, speak powerfully, and model healthy boundaries.

Imagine if every practitioner saw families not as obstacles, but as allies.

What if the primary intervention wasn't always about fixing the person in crisis, but fortifying the people who love them?

This is the shift that will truly turn the tide.

Because while professionals offer hours, families offer presence. While services deliver programs, families deliver moments. It's the look across the table, the words left unsaid, the calm breath in the storm that most often influence the direction of change.

Let us honour that.

Let us teach systems to see what has always been true: healing is collective, and real empowerment begins when we stop trying to rescue the one and start strengthening the circle.

The thought is: What would happen if we gave families the same guidance, the same trust, the same tools? If families were able to connect in a more intentional way, when what I call **Windows of Opportunity** arise—those fleeting moments when a loved one hesitates, reaches, or questions the path they're on.

Imagine if the system recognised that every mother, partner, or sibling who shows up asking, "How can I help them?" isn't just a witness to the crisis, but a lead participant in the solution.

We miss opportunities every day. We underestimate the power of those who already have a relationship with the person struggling. We see them as adjuncts or background noise when in truth, they're the constant.

If we're serious about change, we must start there. The challenge here is to shift the mindset of professionals. Remember, it's easier to do what they've always done, rather than to commit to a different way, not only of thinking but responding.

Empowering families means shifting the message. It's no longer, "Step back and wait."

It becomes:

- ❖ "Here's how to show up differently."
- ❖ "Here's what you can influence."
- ❖ "Here's what matters more than fixing—connecting."

It means giving them permission to be human, make mistakes, and feel rage, grief and confusion, then still come back to the table with curiosity rather than control.

> ***"You don't need to be perfect. You just need to be present. Because change doesn't begin when someone says, 'I'm ready.' It begins when someone feels safe enough to take the first step."***

We've taught families to harden, distance, and detach with love. But what if we also taught them to relate with skill, respond with intention, and hold the line not with anger, but with anchored love?

When we position families as partners, not patients or problems, we begin to restore their agency. We start to rebuild a sense of hope that's rooted in reality. We show them that while they may not control the outcome, they're never powerless.

The bridge isn't built by one person alone; it's built from both sides. And even when your loved one isn't ready or willing to take that first step, you can still lay the foundation. You can steady your end. You can keep the light on, not as a guarantee, but as an act of love and resilience.

The professionals are important. The services matter. But no one holds the key to lasting change more than those who are already in a relationship. When we invest in families through education, support, coaching, and compassion, we activate the most overlooked resource in every system: the people who care the most.

We don't need to professionalise families. We need to equip them. We need to tell them the truth: you're not to blame. You're not powerless. You're not alone. You're not a bystander. You're the keeper of the bridge. And when we give you what you need to hold it steady…you can become an influencer of positive change.

We need to break for these family members whose lives are in chaos, the automatic overwhelming emotional responses, not by years of therapy, but by utilising a therapeutic intervention that can achieve this in as few as three sessions…

> ***"And if families must rediscover their influence, then professionals, too, must remember what truly works. Because wisdom lives not only in the pages of policy, but in the pulse of presence."***

Chapter Three

A NEW WAY OF WORKING

*"The Inner Compass Code™—
a synthesis of subconscious pathways."*

In every culture, long before textbooks and treatment manuals, there were stories. Storytelling wasn't just a means of passing the time; it was the way humans passed on truth. Around fires and under open skies, elders would speak in metaphor, crafting meaning into tales of transformation.

In these stories, a river might represent grief. A storm might be the chaos within. A mountain, the long and personal climb toward clarity. No one needed to explain them. They reached deep into the body, bypassing logic, and spoke straight to the heart and gut. They were healing in motion.

This chapter marks a turning point. It's not just about what works in theory—it's about what has endured across time. *The Inner*

Compass Code™ isn't another model layered on top of broken systems. It's the integration of something ancient with something emerging. It's a way of working that honours wisdom too often dismissed, wisdom passed down in breath, not textbooks.

Over the years, I've walked alongside hundreds of individuals and families navigating the chaos of addiction and behavioural crisis. I've worked in systems designed to help, many of which, despite good intentions, left people feeling more broken. My practice has evolved in response to that reality, shaped by listening, not just to research, but to the knowing within me and the lived experience of those I support.

But I must speak truthfully here. The journey hasn't been easy. I've tried to influence systems and guide practices toward what works. But time and time again, I've hit stonewalls. I've been told I don't fit. That I'm the problem. That my thinking is too deep, too different, too disruptive. I've been praised for my knowledge, then gently (or not so gently) pushed out with a line like, "You should go into research." As though insight and wisdom belong in academic journals, not in the hearts of those on the front lines.

But research has never been my calling. Too many resources are poured into research that leads nowhere real. Data points that have no heartbeat. Findings that help one person once, and then are shelved. Meanwhile, communities suffer. Families crumble. And people are left without the support they truly need.

Let me be clear: Cognitive Behavioural Therapy (CBT) (Beck, 1976) is the most researched model in the Western world. It's structured, measurable, and widely applied. For some, it brings short-term clarity. But in the world of reality, where emotional turmoil, stress, and chaos exist, CBT focuses on the very part of us that's often compromised: the head. The thinking mind. And that, in my view, is the core issue.

You see, for most in distress, it's their head that drives them crazy, it's what keeps them awake at night, it's the part of us that thinks, but it doesn't think clearly. It catastrophises, doubts, rationalises, and denies. It tells convincing stories built on fear, shame, and need. And when we try to treat the distressed or stressed person by addressing only their thoughts, we miss the truth: the mind has been hijacked.

An amazing example of this is the person whose brain is controlled by an addictive behaviour, unhealthy, maladaptive behaviours that cause problems and pain for those who are addicted and their family members. The substance creeps up, infiltrates and takes control of the brain. An 'addicted' brain ensures four things:

1. **There's no choice**—the limbic system is controlled by the unhealthy coping strategy, be that drink or drug or any other maladaptive behaviour. In control, overriding reason.
2. **There's no common sense**—the frontal lobe, responsible for consequence and logic, is offline.
3. **There's no conscience**—core values like "do no harm" are inaccessible.
4. **There's no responsibility**—the addicted brain avoids surrender and refuses accountability, and more importantly, has no desire to give up control!

How, then, can a model rooted in thought correction reach a person whose thoughts are corrupted by compulsion? It cannot. And worse, it trains family and supporters to keep listening to stories that are rooted in dysfunction. I often ask, "How long have you been listening to their story?" The answer is often years. Decades. And then I ask, "Has it helped?" The painful truth is that things have usually gotten worse.

This isn't a failure of will. It's a failure of the model. We don't heal from the head alone. In fact, our tools to create balance in our heads are the hidden treasures we find deeper down. The autonomic nervous system is where we create balance that will rein in the craziness of the head. Simple yet powerful interventions, like balanced breathing, listening to music, taking a walk, meditating, or trying yoga or tai chi.

In contrast, the models that inform ***The Inner Compass Code*™** speak not just to thought, but to story, emotion, memory, body, and spirit. They're grounded in the subconscious, where true transformation occurs:

- ❖ **Neuro-Linguistic Programming (NLP)** (Bandler & Grinder, 1975) shows us how language shapes our internal reality. We reframe not just sentences, but stories and in doing so, shift identity.
- ❖ **Timeline Therapy** (James & Woodsmall, 1988) allows us to heal the past as if it were happening now because to the subconscious, it is. This process echoes ancient rites of storytelling and memory journeys.
- ❖ **Multiple Brain Integration Techniques (mBIT)** (Oka & Soosalu, 2012) remind us that we have three intelligences: head, heart, and gut. Each offers vital wisdom, and only in alignment do we find peace.

- ❖ **The Wheel of Change** (Prochaska & DiClemente, 1983) helps us honour readiness. To roll with resistance and pace readiness for change. Pushing others toward change is often someone else's need, rather than the other person's need; this only feeds continuing resistance.
- ❖ **Motivational Interviewing** (Miller & Rollnick, 1991) teaches us the art of evoking, not enforcing. It holds space for ambivalence and invites movement through gentle reflection.
- ❖ **Relapse Prevention** (Gorski, 1989) and the **12-Step Model** (Alcoholics Anonymous, 2001) offer structure and spirit, combining accountability with community and grace.

These approaches, together, form the navigational tools of **The Inner Compass Code™.** They don't dismiss logic, but they don't worship it. They work with the subconscious, not against it. And they mirror the way traditional cultures have always healed: through story, symbol, reflection, community, and deep reconnection with values.

This work has been deeply influenced by the **Collective Impact Model** (Kania & Kramer, 2011) —a way of creating change not through top-down control, but through community-led transformation, supported by professionals, not dominated by them. It's a return to shared power. To weave wisdom from lived experience into systemic change. This model resonates deeply with my own practice: healing must come from within communities, not be imposed from above.

I've also carried with me a chant born in Aotearoa, New Zealand— my home and foundation. It began as a phrase used when working with Māori, the Indigenous people of the land. And it has become a core truth in all my work:

"What works for Māori, works for Pākehā (people of white skin). But what works for Pākehā does not work for Māori."

This is more than a saying—it's a compass. It reminds us that healing pathways rooted in Indigenous knowledge, community, and connection aren't only valid—they're powerful. And they hold the potential to guide us all.

So yes—this is a new way of working. But it's also the oldest. **The Inner Compass Code**™ is the woven thread between the ancient and the now. It is my life's work. And though I don't share every detail of the journey that led me here, know this: it was hard-won, deeply felt, and tested in the same storm my clients walk through every day.

This chapter is your invitation to step outside the castle of cognitive-only models and into the ever-moving, soul-guided waters of real, lasting change. The journey from chaos to clarity doesn't begin with thought—it begins when we feel the pull of something deeper.

And that, dear reader, is the compass calling you home.

The Next Level of Intervention
My journey has always been away from what doesn't work and toward implementing what does. For me, evidence-based models hold little value, especially when working with those who have already been pulled into the deep end of "expert professional help." Too often, they come away more wounded than supported.

What I do value are models and tools that work in the reality I live and breathe daily—the world of real people, real pain, and real change. Over time, I've grown comfortable being eclectic, drawing from a diverse range of approaches and stripping each one down to the simple, powerful truths at its heart. I've kept only what works.

These tools aren't just techniques. They're energy shifters. They create a connection. They open doors to the inside world, where real answers live. Not the polished answers society wants to hear, but the raw, wise, messy truths that live beneath the surface.

To use these tools effectively, I've discovered three essential milestones—each one a cornerstone in helping someone move from chaos to clarity:

Find Calm First
The number one priority is to reduce stress, turmoil, and chaos. Before anything else, they need calm. But not through years of talk therapy that retraumatises or overexposes. Calm should be achievable in three to six sessions using tools that bypass the conscious mind and work with the body, breath, and subconscious. Traditional "talking cures" may provide temporary relief, but when the next emotional trigger arrives—wham!—they're right back in the storm, acting from impulse, not intention.

Reframe the Problem
Once the nervous system is regulated and calm is present, the next step is mindset. This means questioning what we as a society believe to be true. Because much of what humanity believes… simply isn't true. We must reframe from, "This person is the problem" to, "This behaviour is a response to something deeper." When we can hold space for the messy truth of being human—without accepting harmful behaviours—we start shifting away from blame and toward insight. This opens the door to radical responsibility without shame.

Dismantle the Myth of Individualism and Head Worship
The Western world puts professionals on pedestals. It worships the head. These two things actively disempower people. Humans aren't isolated minds—they're families, communities, and ecosystems. They're relational by design. When someone is seen only as an individual—and worse, only as a diagnosis—they're severed from the very belonging that could support their healing. We must restore connection. People need to feel valued, not viewed as problems to be solved. **The Inner Compass Code**™ does exactly this—it shifts the frame from fixing people to guiding them back to the wisdom already within.

This isn't a theoretical practice. It's lived, embodied, and ever evolving. It respects the sacred in each person. It honours cultural ways of knowing and invites a return to what traditional cultures have always understood: "Healing happens when we're seen, heard, held—and when we remember who we are."

That is the next level of intervention. And it's long overdue.

But if we're to create lasting change, we must also reframe what we value as a Western culture. For too long, success has been measured in things—money, possessions, job titles, and social status. There's nothing inherently wrong with having these things. But when they're valued above all else, we lose sight of what truly sustains us: our well-being, relationships, connection to community and country. It's time we recalibrate our collective compass—not towards power, wealth, or prestige, but toward meaning, belonging, and inner peace.

> *As for man's relentless hunger for power and control... well, that's a tale worthy of its own book.*

Chapter Four

WORDS SHAPE WORLDS – LABELS SHAPE LIVES

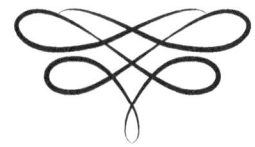

"The language we use can heal...or harm."

Before there were white coats, clipboards, and neatly boxed diagnostic categories, there were stories. Songs. Spoken prayers breathed into the wind and whispered into wounds. Language wasn't clinical. It was sacred. It held the power to shape, summon, honour, or wound. To speak was to shape. To name was to either trap someone in a box...or free them from one.

But over time, language lost its soul. It was systematised, sterilised, and stripped of its humanity. We stopped calling people *hurting* and started calling them *disordered*. We stopped asking *what happened* and began stamping *what's wrong*. As a result, people already drowning in pain were handed labels like anchors, dragging behind them the weight of words they never chose.

In today's systems, to be labelled is often to be locked in. It's a sentence passed down not through understanding, but through assumption.

- "He's in denial."
- "She's not ready to change."
- "They're treatment resistant."

These aren't just phrases—they're pronouncements, and perhaps no one feels their sting more deeply than those walking the long road of trauma.

Take the veteran, handed the diagnosis of post-traumatic stress disorder. For some, it opens doors to support. But for many, it slams shut the windows of possibility. It defines the person, not the pain. It predicts dysfunction rather than honours resilience. And despite years of talking, techniques, and treatments, the flashbacks persist. The fear remains. The pain loops on.

Because what's rarely spoken about in the professional domain is what truly disrupts the cycle: deep, subconscious transformation.

In a world obsessed with talking, we forget that not all healing needs to be verbal. The subconscious doesn't need a diagnosis. It doesn't wait for a case formulation. It responds to process, not analysis. Through techniques grounded in imagination, repetition, and inner permission, we can shift the very patterns that hold trauma in place.

Using what's sometimes called "the trauma cure" in NLP, I've watched people step out of lifelong torment without ever needing to retell their story. All it takes is a word to capture the impact, permission to let it go, and a willingness to follow a guided process that interrupts the rerun tape. 15 minutes. One session. No re-traumatisation. No revisiting old wounds. Just peace—finally unclenched.

And this extends far beyond trauma. Think of how often we slap labels on experiences that are simply amplified emotions: depression—an excess of sadness. Anxiety—an overflow of fear. These aren't lifelong conditions. They're signals. Expressions of overwhelm. And with tools like Timeline Therapy, these emotions can dissolve, often within minutes.

Yet these methods remain unfunded, unseen by mainstream systems. Why? Because the system has grown to serve itself. It clings to the known, the measurable, the formulaic—even if the outcomes continue to fail.

And so we must also speak of power. Man's unrelenting hunger for control echoes not just in politics, but in professional hierarchies. Degrees become armour. Titles become shields. Behind them, some experts become untouchable.

"This is the right way."

"Your method isn't evidence-based."

"Change takes time."

But whose evidence? And whose clock are we running on?

True expertise should be a bridge, not a barricade. A lighthouse, not a fortress. Yet too often, it becomes an ivory tower guarded by acronyms and blind to the wisdom found in lived experience, community, and intuitive knowing.

This chapter is a call to rise. A call to those ready to speak differently, listen more deeply, and act with courage. A call to those who've tasted freedom and now long to pass that gift on. Because words shape worlds. Labels shape lives. Let us choose a language that sets people free.

And now, let us turn our gaze to those standing beside the storm—the mothers, fathers, sisters, partners. The ones who have loved, pleaded, sacrificed, and often lost themselves trying to save someone else.

They, too, have been labelled: *enablers*, *codependents*, *part of the problem*. But here, we offer a new truth. They're gardeners. Caretakers of sacred soil. Their role isn't to force growth, but to nurture it. To plant intentional seeds during Windows of Opportunity.

But these seeds must be planted with wisdom. With words that inspire *responsibility*, not guilt. With a presence that steps *back*, not away, but far enough to let roots take hold. Because when we smother change with our own fear, need, and urgency, we cast a shadow over what's trying to grow. The seed may still be there, but it cannot reach the light.

Families are powerful users of language. Every word they speak can reinforce a cycle—or quietly, steadily, break one. Yet too often, in desperation, they speak too many words. They lecture.

They correct. They point out brokenness. But the truth is this: when someone is drowning, what they need isn't a commentary on how they got there—they need a clear space to surface.

Less is more. Few words, spoken with conviction, carry far greater weight than a thousand said in fear. Saying, "I can see you're trying," can build more momentum than any long-winded advice ever could.

It's not about giving answers. It's about affirming the little things, like their accomplishments, insight and desire for change. Holding your own boundaries, being aligned with your values, role modelling, building a healthy relationship with self, doing no harm to self (or others), respecting self (and others); this stuff in action is powerful—no words needed.

You can have zero tolerance for abuse by honouring your own boundaries, taking care of your needs and being true to them. Separating the person from the problem means no longer putting the person at the centre as the problem. Connecting with the person, having acceptance of their humanness, is powerful, and valuing the person underneath the pain is empowering for all.

See their strength, believe in their ability to solve their own problems, stop saving them from consequences and accept the spiritual journey we're all on. This is God's will, not my own.

Remember, you cannot 'talk' the person into a different perspective on self—you cannot talk the person into more healthy coping strategies, and you certainly cannot talk the person into accepting it's okay to feel not okay. Resilience will grow, and the relationship with self will shift when others are allowed to walk their journey and grow beyond the need for alcohol or drugs in their life. When you can step back and offer words of reassurance, and allow them to take responsibility for their actions, change will have the opportunity to begin.

Support, at its most powerful, sounds like this:
Jack has had another horror high-risk binge. He sits with his head low, just waiting for the words of destruction, his mother's bitter disappointment, his father's anger. His Mum and Dad look at each other before Dad plants a very powerful seed, "Jack, I'm wondering if this is the way you want to live the rest of your life?" No answer needed, no more said, that seed is now planted, and Jack will think about it when the time is right.

Julie is feeling lost and alone. Her sisters don't want her around, and her family has virtually disowned her. She's totally broken, barely able to function with her substance of choice.

She mutters to her mother, "I'm sick of how everyone hates me, no one cares."

Her mother has the urge to tell her they don't hate her, they do care but remembers this is reality for Julie. Mum knows her words cannot change that; she has tried a thousand times before. She looks at Julie and quietly says, "I care," adding, "I'm wondering what you may want to do to change this for you."

No answer needed, no more said, that seed is now planted, and Julie will think about it when the time is right.

Let that be the final power of our words—not spoken in fear, but in faith. Not to control, but to invite. Not to save, but to set free.

"Because when we speak from love, with strength and restraint, we don't just offer hope. We offer a mirror for the change they must choose to see in themselves."

Chapter Five

THE FIRE WITHIN

"A call to professionals to lead the change."

There comes a time in every storm-tossed journey when a question must rise from the depths: Will I keep circling the same waters, or will I chart a new course?

This is the invitation at the heart of this final chapter—not just to reflect, but to act. Not merely to think differently, but to become different. Not just to know there's another way, but to commit to walking it. To rise not as professionals following the system's tide, but as change-makers choosing to redirect it.

Professionals can reach more families, empowering them through a different response, to change the tide. You may be at the edge of exhaustion, your spirit worn thin by years inside a system that preaches care yet often delivers compliance—this is your call to rise. To remember. To reimagine. To reconnect with why you entered this work to begin with, and who you once hoped to become inside it.

For those who have walked beside the broken—families, clients, communities—this isn't a suggestion. It's a summons. A call to professionals to reimagine how we practise, to reframe what support truly means, and to rebuild the path forward. Not by tearing everything down, but by becoming living proof that a new way is possible—even inside a broken system.

Because let's speak plainly: the pain of this work isn't just felt by those receiving it. It lives in the hearts of those who chose this profession to make a difference, only to discover that the system itself often stands in the way. Somewhere between intake forms and outcome targets, the soul of your practice got buried.

But it's not lost. And your fire, though dimmed, still burns. The embers are waiting.

The Inner Compass Code™ isn't a product. It's not a workshop or a weekend retreat. It's a reclamation. A return. A remembering of what was once known in the bones, breath, and collective hum of community. That healing is relational. That wisdom is embodied. That connection—not correction—is what changes lives.

This code doesn't ignore evidence—it deepens it. It doesn't abandon practice—it awakens it. It doesn't replace structure—it infuses it with soul. It offers a path where professionals—social workers, therapists, caseworkers, youth mentors, community leaders—can finally work in a way that honours both their training and their truth.

A path that says: you don't have to choose between professionalism and humanity. You can lead with compassion and be effective. You can hold power with people, not over them. You don't have to fix people. You're not supposed to.

What if your real work was to become a mirror—one that reflects possibility, not deficiency? What if your true role was to hold the map steady, not to walk the path for others, but to walk beside them, with reverence?

Your Inner Compass doesn't shout. It doesn't bark orders from the brain like a military commander. It emerges when the noise quiets—when the head, heart, and gut fall into alignment. You'll know you're living from your Inner Compass when your energy feels clear. When you speak and something inside you says, *That's true*. When your presence becomes medicine without saying a word.

It feels like groundedness without control. Boundaries without guilt. Stillness in the chaos. The quiet courage to act with integrity, even when systems pull you elsewhere. When the head balances the heart. When the gut stands firm. When the spirit aligns your why with your how—that's when the Compass is leading. You're no longer scattered. You're no longer surviving. You're living, leading, and loving with your whole being.

So many good people are hurting in this field. Not because they don't care, but because they care too deeply. You've seen the harm of broken systems. You've witnessed band-aids slapped on gaping wounds. You've been asked to chart progress while the soul of the work slips through the cracks.

If you've ever been told, "You're too emotional."

"Stick to the script."

"That's not your job."

Then **The Inner Compass Code**™ is for you. Within you, something rises. A fierce knowing. A rebel whisper. A sacred refusal to become numb. That whisper is your Inner Compass; it's guiding you toward something powerful, something great.

I want you to know—you're not alone. There's a collective rising. A movement of professionals refusing to trade their purpose for a pay cheque. Professionals who are ready to bring wisdom back into the work, to sit in sacred discomfort, and to build new ways in the bones of the old.

This is more than a framework. It's the beginning of a revolution.

Through my professional development path—Reimagine, Reframe & Rebuild—we walk together, not as cogs in the system, but as keepers of the flame. We reimagine what this work could be—not by seeking permission, but by reclaiming power. We reframe who we are—not as rescuers, but as presence-filled practitioners who influence change through alignment, not authority.

We rebuild practice from the inside out—not with more policies, but with more humanity. This isn't about learning a method. It's about finding your fire. You'll walk away not with a manual, but with a map and the trust in yourself to follow it. You'll connect with others who are also daring to believe that relationship is the medicine. That presence is the practice. That heart isn't a liability—it's the key.

This isn't a solo journey. It was never meant to be. **The Inner Compass Code**™ isn't only about personal alignment—it's about collective restoration. About remembering what ancient cultures knew before colonisation fractured our ways of being. That healing happens in community. That power is shared, not seized. That wisdom lives not in institutions, but in the in-between—in circle, in ceremony, in relationship.

We're not here to replicate systems. We're here to reweave what was torn. To walk alongside, not above. To hold space for truths that don't fit into intake boxes or ticked charts. This is how we reclaim the future—by becoming the bridge between what was and what will be.

Together, we're remembering. Together, we're rebuilding. And if these words have touched something buried—something tired, something fierce, something true—then this isn't your invitation. It's your moment. Don't wait for permission. Don't wait for funding. Don't wait for someone else to lead. The fire is already within you.

Your next step isn't optional—it's necessary. It's now. For those who are still wondering where the research is, where is the evidence, I want to share with you a short story.

The Old Tree and the Scholar

There was once a great scholar who had studied all the sciences of the world. His shelves were heavy with papers, journals, and research that spoke of cause and effect, input and output. He had learned to trust what could be measured. What could be published. What could be proven.

And still, he felt empty.

One day, weary of his own knowing, he climbed a mountain in search of a famous old tree—a tree that, they said, held the kind of wisdom that couldn't be written down.

When he found it, he stood before its enormous trunk, wrapped in moss and silence. Its roots were so deep they split the stone. Its leaves whispered in a language not taught in books. The scholar circled it for hours. He measured its width. He noted its species. He counted its rings.

*Then he sat at its base and asked aloud,
"What makes you so wise?"*

The tree said nothing.

*So the scholar asked again. This time, with a slight edge:
"Where is your research? Where is your peer review?"*

The wind rustled. A leaf drifted down and landed beside him.

The tree still said nothing.

*He waited until the silence began to fray his logic.
Until he could no longer bear the absence of data.*

And then a woman appeared—old, like the tree itself. She watched him with kind eyes.

"What are you looking for?" she asked.

"Proof," he replied. "That this tree is as wise as they say. That there's reason to trust it."

The woman nodded and sat beside him. "And in all your learning," she asked gently, "did you ever find a paper that taught you how to love?"

He blinked. "No."

"Did a study ever hold you when you broke?"

"No."

"Did your citations bring you comfort when your heart was tired of pretending to be strong?"

"No."

She looked up at the tree. "Then maybe you already know this: the deepest truths do not need defending. They only need remembering."

The scholar stared at the leaf that had fallen beside him. It was small. inconsequential, perhaps. But it carried the tree's entire code inside it.

He bowed his head.

And for the first time in his life, he stopped thinking.

And began to listen.

Let that be the wisdom that greets those still seeking evidence:
There's a knowing deeper than knowledge.

There's a truth that outlives textbooks.

There's a code written not in journals, but in breath, blood, presence, and practice.

You already know it. You've felt it. Now, it's time to live it.

It's the beginning of the end of systems as we know them—and the start of something that will burn brighter, stand taller, and reach deeper than anything we've done before. Step forward. The conclusion awaits.

Conclusion

THE COMPASS IS YOURS NOW

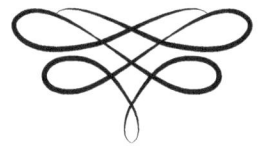

You made it here.

Not just to the end of a book, but to the edge of a tide you cannot unsee. A tide of change, of truth, of something ancient rising through the cracks of modern systems.

We began with silence, with pain, with a woman standing on a footpath believing her journey was over. I wasn't alright. Not even close. But the story didn't end there. Because from that moment of almost-ending came a slow return—a reawakening. Not just to life, but to soul. To knowing. To the pulse of a deeper truth that lives beneath the noise of our broken world.

This book has carried you through that journey. It has walked you through my own unravelling, and perhaps, held up a mirror to your own. Along the way, we've called out systems, reclaimed language, challenged models, and laid bare the quiet harm done when heart is sacrificed in the name of professionalism.

And now, standing here with you, I ask not for analysis or agreement.

I offer something older, wilder, and more sacred.

An ode.

To those who have sailed these wild seas…
To those who drowned before they ever reached the shore…
To those who fought the current with everything they had…
To those who still clutch driftwood, praying the waves will still…
To those who reached safe harbour, soaked but standing…

This is for you.

*And this—***The Inner Compass Code***™—isn't just mine.*
It's yours now, too.
Carved from wind and wave, it carries the wisdom I couldn't hold alone.
In the world of my app and the community that follows it, we don't speak in prescriptions.
We speak in tides.
In ports of call.
In storms broken and compasses found.
We remember that healing isn't linear, it's tidal.
And we honour the messiness, the salt, the scars left by survival.
So, as you stand now at this book's end, know this: you're not standing at a conclusion.
You're standing at a new beginning.
And the choice before you is no longer whether to sail.
It's how.

Broken Families, Broken Systems, Broken Promises
The Compass Is Yours Now

With your Compass in hand, your heart steady,
and your knowing awakened—step forward.
You've read the pages.
You've felt the fire.
Now you must choose.
To carry this into your practice.
Into your relationships.
Into your systems, your circles, your shorelines.
To become the lighthouse for those still adrift.
Because the world doesn't need more professionals.
It needs more wayfinders.
And the sea is calling.

ABOUT THE AUTHOR

Rosemary Brown is no stranger to the storm of addiction, mental health, and a chaotic system that falls short for those who need it. Since 1999, she has stood at the crossroads of broken families, fractured systems, and shattered promises, offering not just professional expertise but a fierce, unwavering commitment to change.

As an addiction and behaviour change specialist, Rosemary is the creator of **The Inner Compass Code**™. She has worked alongside those individuals and families affected the most by addiction, trauma, and systemic failure.

But Rosemary's journey is not merely one of academic knowledge or clinical practice. Her's is a lived journey, carved from personal trials, raw truth, and a relentless search for answers when the systems meant to help fell silent. Her work rises from the deep conviction that real change begins within, and that families, not institutions, hold the greatest power to heal what addiction and broken systems have left behind.

In **Broken Families, Broken Systems, Broken Promises,** Rosemary weaves together personal narrative, professional insight, and the ancient threads of Traditional Wisdom to challenge outdated models and ignite a new movement of practice.

This book is not only a call to families but a stirring invitation to professionals, offering pathways to work differently, integrate

***The Inner Compass Code*^{TM}** into their own practices, and become catalysts for the kind of change that transforms not just individuals but entire systems.

Through her digital programs, coaching platform, and app— Alcohol, Drugs & Change – by Rosemary Brown—Rosemary empowers professionals and families alike to reclaim their strength, align with timeless principles, and chart a new course toward meaningful, lasting change.

An Invitation to Professionals

If you're a professional standing at the edge of frustration, exhausted by systems that fail, desperate for a better way, and yearning to bring real, soul-deep transformation to the people you serve, this invitation is for you.

***The Inner Compass Code*^{TM}** is more than a framework. It's a living, breathing system drawn from Traditional Wisdom, professional expertise, and hard-won experience. It has been shaped not only by Rosemary Brown's own journey but by the countless families and individuals whose stories pulse through its core.

While born from the world of addiction and family change, **The Inner Compass Code^{TM}** reaches far beyond. Its tools and principles are designed for anyone who supports others in achieving positive change, whether you work in counselling, coaching, social services, education, health, or human development.

For the first time, professionals are invited to train directly with Rosemary and gain the right to become an endorsed, registered

***Inner Compass Code*ᵀᴹ** *Professional.* This is your chance to work differently with tools that move beneath the surface, empowering those you serve to reclaim their direction and create lasting transformation.

If you're ready to deepen your practice and join a movement to reshape the future of human change, we invite you to express your interest today.

Email rosemary@theinnercompasscode.com to begin the conversation.

The revolution is waiting for you. Will you answer the call?

An Invitation to Speak

Rosemary Brown is a powerhouse voice in the fields of family transformation, addiction, and systemic change. As the creator of ***The Inner Compass Code*ᵀᴹ**—a groundbreaking system blending Traditional Wisdom, lived experience, and professional expertise—Rosemary brings a rare, compelling mix of deep insight, practical strategy, and heartfelt connection to every stage and platform she steps onto.

With decades of frontline experience, Rosemary has worked alongside thousands of individuals and many of their family members too, advocating for a new, soul-driven approach that empowers families and communities, not just systems. She's the author of ***Broken Families, Broken Systems, Broken Promises*** and the founder of **Alcohol, Drugs & Change – by Rosemary Brown,** a coaching platform transforming how people approach personal and relational change.

Rosemary's talks are known for their raw honesty, warmth, and ability to ignite fresh thinking. Whether speaking to professionals, families, or the wider community, she delivers clarity, passion, and a rallying cry for change that resonates long after the event ends.

Invitation:
Rosemary is available to speak on podcasts, at conferences, and at community events—anywhere people are gathering to explore new ways forward in creating positive, lasting change.

To invite Rosemary to speak, **email rosemary@theinnercompasscode.com** and begin the conversation.

Together, let's spark a new era of hope, wisdom, and possibility in our communities.

An Invitation to Organisations: Reenergise Your Staff with *The Inner Compass Code*™

If you're a leader within an organisation committed to creating meaningful, lasting change—whether in addiction services, social care, education, health, justice, or human development—**The Inner Compass Code**™ offers a groundbreaking opportunity to retrain your team.

This isn't just another professional development course. This is a transformational retraining experience designed to reshape how your staff engage with the people they serve. Drawing on Traditional Wisdom, frontline experience, and a system honed through decades of practice, **The Inner Compass Code**™ equips professionals with tools that move beyond surface solutions, unlocking profound, client-led change.

Your staff will not only gain new strategies—they'll gain a new lens through which to understand their work, clients, and themselves. By completing this retraining, they can become endorsed **Inner Compass Code**™ *Professionals*, recognised by Rosemary Brown and positioned at the forefront of a movement committed to doing things differently.

For organisations ready to invest in a workforce that leads with purpose, wisdom, and impact, this is your moment.

To explore organisational reenergising options, email rosemary@theinnercompasscode.com to arrange a conversation.

Let's reimagine the future of service—together.

DISCLAIMER

Our training and coaching products, including **The Inner Compass Code**™ and related materials, are designed to offer tools, guidance, and support to assist you on your journey of growth and change. However, we do not guarantee specific outcomes or results.

Your progress and success depend on a range of factors unique to you—including your personal circumstances, the time you devote, your level of engagement, and the commitment you bring to the process. As with any transformational work, outcomes will vary greatly between individuals, and results are influenced by many factors beyond our control.

We encourage you to approach this journey with an open heart, a curious mind, and a steady commitment, knowing that meaningful change unfolds uniquely for everyone.

The revolution begins here.

REFERENCES

AIATSIS. (2020). *Code of ethics for Aboriginal and Torres Strait Islander research*. Australian Institute of Aboriginal and Torres Strait Islander Studies. https://aiatsis.gov.au/code-ethics

Alcoholics Anonymous. (2001). *Alcoholics Anonymous: The story of how many thousands of men and women have recovered from alcoholism* (4th ed.). Alcoholics Anonymous World Services. (Original work published 1939)

Arrien, A. (1993). *The Four-Fold Way: Walking the paths of the warrior, teacher, healer, and visionary*. HarperSanFrancisco.

Australian Bureau of Statistics. (2008). *National Survey of Mental Health and Wellbeing: Summary of Results*. ABS Catalogue No. 4326.0.

Australian Bureau of Statistics. (2023). *Personal Safety Survey, Australia*. ABS Catalogue No. 4906.0.

Australian Bureau of Statistics. (2024). *Causes of Death, Australia*. ABS Catalogue No. 3303.0.

Australian Institute of Health and Welfare. (2005). *Australia's Health 2004*. AIHW Catalogue No. AUS 44.

Australian Institute of Health and Welfare. (2015). *Australia's Health 2014*. AIHW Catalogue No. AUS 178.

Australian Institute of Health and Welfare. (2022). *Elder abuse: Understanding issues, frameworks and responses*. AIHW.

Australian Institute of Health and Welfare. (2023). *Alcohol, tobacco & other drugs in Australia*. https://www.aihw.gov.au/reports/alcohol/alcohol-tobacco-other-drugs-australia

Australian Institute of Health and Welfare. (2024). *National Drug Strategy Household Survey 2022: Detailed findings*.

Bandler, R., & Grinder, J. (1975). *The structure of magic: A book about language and therapy*. Science and Behavior Books.

Beck, A. T. (1976). *Cognitive therapy and the emotional disorders*. International Universities Press.

Commonwealth of Australia. (2022). *National Plan to End Violence against Women and Children 2022–2032*. Department of Social Services. https://www.dss.gov.au/national-plan

Commonwealth of Australia. (2023). *Mental Health Services in Australia: Expenditure and performance snapshot*. Department of Health and Aged Care.

Durie, M. (1985). *A Māori perspective of health*. Paper presented at the 4th New Zealand Medical Association Conference, Auckland, New Zealand.

Gee, G., Dudgeon, P., Schultz, C., Hart, A., & Kelly, K. (2014). Aboriginal and Torres Strait Islander social and emotional wellbeing. In P. Dudgeon, H. Milroy, & R. Walker (Eds.), *Working together: Aboriginal and Torres Strait Islander mental health and wellbeing principles and practice* (2nd ed., pp. 55–68). Commonwealth of Australia.

Gorski, T. T. (1989). *Passages through recovery: An action plan for preventing relapse*. HarperOne.

James, T., & Woodsmall, W. (1988). *Time Line Therapy and the basis of personality*. Meta Publications.

Kania, J., & Kramer, M. (2011). Collective impact. *Stanford Social Innovation Review*, 9(1), 36–41. https://doi.org/10.48558/n9g3-pb91

Miller, W. R., & Rollnick, S. (1991). *Motivational interviewing: Preparing people to change addictive behaviour*. Guilford Press.

Mission Australia & Black Dog Institute. (2024). *Youth Survey Report 2024*.

Ngaanyatjarra Pitjantjatjara Yankunytjatjara Women's Council Aboriginal Corporation. (2013). *Ngankari Work—Anangu Way: Traditional Healers of Central Australia*. NPY Women's Council.

Oka, M., & Soosalu, G. (2012). *mBraining: Using your multiple brains to do cool stuff*. mBIT International Pty Ltd.

Prochaska, J. O., & DiClemente, C. C. (1983). *Stages and processes of self-change of smoking: Toward an integrative model of change*. Journal of Consulting and Clinical Psychology, 51(3), 390–395.

Stanner, W. E. H. (1979). *White man got no dreaming: Essays 1938–1973*. Australian National University Press.

Ungunmerr-Baumann, M. R. (2002). *Dadirri: Listening to one another*. In D. Dudgeon, M. Huygens & L. Walker (Eds.), *Speaking from the heart: Indigenous voices on mental health and wellbeing* (pp. 183–186). Hawker Brownlow Education.

NOTES

Broken Families, Broken Systems, Broken Promises
Notes

Broken Families, Broken Systems, Broken Promises
Notes

www.ingramcontent.com/pod-product-compliance
Lightning Source LLC
Chambersburg PA
CBHW061218070526
44584CB00029B/3883